M000251181

ALSO BY ALLEN W. SMITH

The Looting of Social Security

Social Security: The Attempt to Kill It

The Big Lie

RAIDING THE TRUST FUND

Using Social Security Money to Fund Tax Cuts for the Rich

Allen W. Smith, Ph.D.

ISBN 978-0-9903036-6-4

To Joan

CONTENTS

CHAPTER ONE

INTRODUCTION

The starting point of this story dates back 32 years to April 20, 1983 when President Ronald Reagan signed the Social Security Amendments of 1983 into law with great fanfare. He called them, "landmark legislation," and made glowing remarks about what he thought the legislation had accomplished:

> Our elderly need no longer fear that the checks they depend on will be stopped or reduced. These amendments protect them. Americans of middle age need no longer worry whether their career-long investment will pay off. These amendments guarantee it.

I did not become a part of the story until 17 years later, when on a warm September morning in 2000 I was sitting at my desk in my Naples home when the phone rang. I picked up and the pleasant female voice on the other end asked,

"Are you Dr. Allen W. Smith?"

I assured her that I was.

"This is CNN News in Atlanta," she said.

I had never received a call from CNN, or any other news organization, so I just assumed they were conducting a poll or survey.

"We've had a last minute cancellation for the two o'clock news today," the polite caller said,

"And we were wondering if you could appear instead. We have your book here, and, if you could get to our studio in Fort Myers in time for the two o'clock news, we'd like to have you as a guest."

I had sent complimentary review copies of my new self-published book, "The Alleged Budget Surplus, Social Security and Voodoo Economics," so I wasn't surprised that CNN had a copy. But I was shocked, and thrilled, at the prospect they might want me to talk about the book on the air.

The call stemmed from an important discovery I had made several months earlier while doing some research. I discovered, to my astonishment, that the surplus Social Security revenue, which was supposed to be saved and invested in marketable U.S. Treasury bonds for the eventual baby boomers' retirement, was being improperly used. The money was not being saved. Instead, it was being used to fund general government operations.

My first clue to this came from a short pamphlet I found, written by an employee of the Social Security Administration. And that spilled a lot of beans! It stated that the Social Security money was being spent just like income tax revenue, and it was being replaced by putting non-marketable IOUs in the Social Security trust fund. As if this were not bad enough, the pamphlet alleged that the interest the government was supposedly paying on its debt to Social Security was being "paid" in the form of more of the same worthless IOUs—not cash.

At first, I doubted all this was true. It was just too shocking. Surely our government could not be using money, which had been collected exclusively for Social Security, to pay other bills. My first thought was that the pamphlet might have been written as a joke. But it didn't take much further research to discover that I had just stumbled onto a massive fraud.

A quick review of the Congressional Record showed that as early as 1989, Senator Ernest Hollings (D-SC) had referred to the IOU's in the trust fund as a "21st Century version of Confederate Bank notes."

And, in 1990, Senator Harry Reid (D-NV) had stated in a speech in the Senate, "We have been stealing money from the Social Security recipients of this country."

The government was indeed spending Social Security money on other programs in 2000, and, outside the government, almost no one seemed to know about it.

As I approached the TV station in Fort Myers, my mind was running in circles. Once I had become absolutely sure that this was really going on, I had begun writing a new book about this scam in detail. I feared I had no time to search for an agent or publisher. This was hot, and the public had to be alerted immediately. So I self-published the book and had it out by early September.

As we parked outside the TV station, I thought I was now about to get lucky. Once CNN reported my story, it would be big breaking news, and the word would explode out to the public. But I was so naïve about the nature of the news media at that time. It was so different from the media that had exposed Watergate during the Nixon presidency.

As I sat in the TV Studio, preparing for my first ever appearance on national television, I was too excited to be nervous. I would soon tell millions of people about the Social Security scam.

Once the time arrived, I found myself staring into a monitor at the face of Lou Waters, the CNN anchor in Atlanta. And I was ready to expose the Social Security fraud.

But the interview didn't go the way I had hoped.

Waters introduced me by saying, "The person you're about to meet might accuse the federal government of economic malpractice. He is economist Allen Smith, who says there is no surplus, that it's all a big, fat myth."

I tried my heart out to convince Waters that Social Security money was being spent for other programs. But he would have no part of it.

Below are excerpts from the transcript of the interview:

WATERS: You're saying that this money that we're hearing is a government surplus that we're paying down the federal debt with is Social Security money?

SMITH: It is Social Security money, and they are not paying down the debt.

WATERS: So we're being misled by the politicians with all these campaign promises?

SMITH: We are being totally deceived. I think this is the biggest deception in American history.

WATERS: Is there a danger for the future?

SMITH: There is a big danger because our economy right now is healthy, extremely healthy, but the budget of the United States government is probably the worst it's ever been in terms of indebtedness.

Waters seemed more amused than interested in what I was saying, and finally he said,

"We're not hearing any of this in the news. I'm involved in the news. Are you a voice crying in the wilderness?"

As things turned out, I was a voice crying in the wilderness on September 27, 2000. But I had spelled out the fraud in detail in my new book, and people would soon know about it, I naively thought.

I've always been troubled by social injustice, and it appeared that this might be the greatest of all time. Social Security contributions, from working Americans, were being used to help finance the large Reagan income tax cuts. Cuts, which went disproportionately to the rich. The 1982 Commission on Social Security Reform, and the Social Security Amendments of 1983 were scams against the American public.

As we drove back to Naples, I was excited, and a plan began to emerge in my mind. I vowed that I would not rest until the Social Security scam was exposed, and those responsible were held accountable.

As my mind jumped from thought to thought, I realized that I needed to talk to my wife, Joan, about one idea that kept popping into my mind, uninvited.

"Sweetie," I said cautiously. "I want to ask you something."

"Okay," she responded, "What is it?"

"I'm thinking about borrowing money to promote the book."

"How much?" she asked.

I don't know. But we won't sell many copies if people don't know the book exists. And if the book doesn't sell, the money we've already spent printing the books will be wasted."

"That doesn't make sense," Joan said.

"It's just that it's such an important issue," I said. "I want to get the word out as soon as possible."

When we got home that afternoon, life wasn't quite the same. Earlier that morning, everything was normal. But that phone call, and the trip to Fort Myers to do the interview, had changed things, at least a bit. For the next few days, I did a lot of soul searching. My life was better than I'd ever dreamed it could be. So I didn't want to mess things up.

A few days after the CNN interview, Joan and I went to Caribbean Gardens, our favorite place in the Naples area. We had season passes to the beautiful botanical gardens, and we tried to go at least once a week. We had a favorite spot in the gardens, near a small pond, that was lined with palm trees and surrounded by a large grassy area. Joan and I liked to go to our special spot whenever we wanted to do some serious thinking or talking, and that's what we needed to do that afternoon.

As we sat on the grass, gazing at the beautiful pond and the lovely palm trees, swaying in the gentle breeze, it seemed inappropriate to drag a big problem into that tranquil place. So we just soaked in the sights and sounds for a few minutes before even thinking about what we would soon be discussing.

It had been a few days since the interview, and we had a better perspective on the situation than on the day of the interview. We reminded ourselves that the interview came only because another guest had cancelled at the last minute. But, it had happened. I had told a large national audience about the Social Security scam, and I hungered for more opportunities to expose the fraud.

We considered the options we had for promoting the book, and we both wanted to do something big.

"What if we placed a full-page ad in a major national magazine?" I asked.

"I don't know," Joan said. "It would cost a lot of money, and we couldn't be sure that anyone would even read it."

"Yeah, you're probably right," I said. "But just spending small amounts here and there probably won't do any good either. We need a way to reach a lot of people."

We finally decided to gamble big time. We borrowed $4,000 to place a full-page, four-color ad in *The New Republic*. The ad appeared in the October 9, 2000 issue— the one with the cover photo of George W. Bush, kissing Oprah on the cheek. I still have that magazine. I keep it to remind me of the $4,000 ad, which accomplished almost nothing. It was the closest I had ever come to playing the lottery, and I vowed to be a lot more careful how I spent money in the future.

On January 20, 1983, the Greenspan Commission on Social Security Reform had sent its recommendations to the President and the Congress. The proposed legislation was rushed through Congress in only three months, and, on April 20, 1983, President Reagan signed the legislation into law.

At the signing ceremony, Reagan had made it sound like April 20, 1983 would go down in history as a proud day for America. And, ironically, even to this day, the myth that Democratic House Speaker Tip O'Neill and Republican President Ronald Reagan "solved the Social Security crisis of 1983," still persists. But it was all a big lie. The 1983 legislation enabled the government to embezzle and spend $2.7 trillion that belonged to the trust fund and to the workers who had contributed to it.

The baby boomers were the reason for the 1983 legislation. The Greenspan Commission had found that there were no major financing problems for Social Security in the short term. The only major problem on the horizon was the forthcoming retirement of the baby boomers, some 30 years down the road. A tiny tax increase might have been warranted. But there was no justification for enacting a large tax increase to solve a problem that was decades away.

Nevertheless, Reagan and Greenspan convinced Congress to take action on the future financing problem that would exist when the baby boomers retired. The plan called for a hefty payroll tax hike on the baby boomers. In addition to paying for the cost of their parents' benefits, the boomers were required to pay enough additional taxes to prepay their own benefits. As a result, the baby boomers have contributed more to Social Security than any other generation.

The higher taxes were designed to generate large Social Security surpluses for the next thirty years. The surplus revenue was supposed to be saved and invested in marketable U.S. Treasury bonds. The Treasury bonds would later be sold to raise cash with which to pay benefits to the boomers.

What should've been seen as a red flag was that the legislation called for imposing large tax increases, effective immediately, to deal with a problem that was 30 years away. That is just not the way the United States has traditionally done things. By nature, we are a crisis nation. We usually don't take action on a major problem until it's almost too late. So why did the government raise taxes in 1983 when the money wouldn't be needed for 30 years?

Reagan needed general revenue to replace the lost revenue from his unaffordable income-tax cuts. Instead of moving closer to a balanced budget, which Reagan had promised we would have by 1984, we had exploding federal budget deficits and a doubling of the national debt . from $1 trillion in 1981 to $2 trillion six years later.

Supply-side economics wasn't working the way Reagan had said it would work, so additional revenue was desperately needed. Reagan could have just admitted that he'd been wrong about the tax cuts, and he could've proposed rescinding a large portion of them. But that was not in his nature. He had to find another way to keep the deficits down.

When the first significant revenue from the 1983 payroll tax hike arrived at the U.S. Treasury in 1985, instead of setting it aside for the baby boomers, the money was quietly deposited directly into the general fund.

There was a Social Security surplus of $9.4 billion in 1985, with increasingly larger annual surpluses thereafter. In total, the 1983 payroll tax hike had generated $2.7 trillion in surplus revenue by the time the annual surpluses ended in 2010. That is how much Social Security money has been used to fund wars and other government programs. That is how much the government now owes to the Social Security trust fund.

As part of my effort to expose the Social Security fraud, I began to advertise my availability for radio interviews via telephone in Radio-TV Interview Report. I got quite a few interviews through the ads, and I paid a large PR firm, to schedule additional interviews for me with some of the bigger radio stations. I have done more than 200 radio interviews about Social Security with stations, both large and small, all over the country.

My goal of getting another book on Social Security published, was achieved when New York publisher, Carroll & Graf, released, "THE LOOTING OF SOCIAL SECURITY: How The Government Is Draining America's Retirement Account," in early 2004. I was elated. I thought I had almost reached the promised land. After four years of frustration in my efforts to expose the Social

Security theft, I finally had a book, published by a regular publisher, that I thought would finally expose the awful truth about the trust fund.

When the book first came out, I was confident that it would reach a large audience. But events over the next few months showed just how wrong I was. The first hint of trouble was a lengthy UPI.com article, about me and the book, written by Paul W. Robberson. The article/review appeared in the Business section of the Washington Times on January 27, 2004.

To give the reader a feel for the nature of the article/review, I am reproducing the first three paragraphs below:

> "Screaming 'Fire! Fire!' when smoke is detected in a crowded room may be the prudent thing to do, but what about an author who stridently writes 'Fraud! Fraud!' about the operation of the Social Security system, when, in fact, the U.S. government is spending the money according to rules enacted by Congress.

> If fraud has occurred, then someone must be brought to justice, but if the claim is manufactured or embellished, then someone has been falsely accused.

> Allen W. Smith does just that in '*The Looting of Social Security*' (Carroll and Graf Publishers, New York, 2004, $11.20 paperback, 256 pp). Smith unleashes his attack with the bold salvo that President George W. Bush is "participating in massive fraud against the American public."

The above excerpt is only about 10 percent of the "review." Mr. Robberson rants on for more than 1100 words. Near the end he writes:

> "Clearly Smith is no fan of Bush, his father, his family, or his friends, and he uses his poorly constructed looting indictment as the vehicle for his venting."

I was flattered that the right-wing Washington Times would devote 1100 words to me and my book. But, I felt almost sure they had an ulterior motive for doing so. I saw the article as a warning to conservatives that a book exposing the Social Security fraud was about to be published.

A month later, on February 25, 2004, Alan Greenspan launched a verbal bombshell, which set off anger, and some degree of panic, throughout the nation. Social Security had not received much public attention since the "fix" of 1983, and most Americans were confident that the program was fiscally sound. Thus, Greenspan's call for trimming Social Security benefits for future retirees touched a nerve in many Americans.

Testifying before the House Budget Committee, Greenspan said:

> We are over committed at this stage. It is important that we tell people who are about to retire what it is they will have.

Greenspan pointed to the forthcoming retirement of the baby-boom generation as the reason for his concern.

> "This dramatic demographic change is certain to place enormous demands on our nation's resources—demands we will almost surely be unable to meet unless action is taken."

I was furious over Greenspan's double-crossing of the baby boomers. In 1983, Greenspan had argued that we needed to raise taxes on the baby boomers so they would prepay most of the costs of their own benefits. That was the whole point of the Social Security Amendments of

1983! Taxes were raised to build up a large reserve surplus in the trust fund so there would be enough money for the baby boomers' retirement. That money had been stolen by the government and spent on other things, and Greenspan was pretending that the money had never been there.

Surprisingly, I had the unexpected opportunity to vent my anger directly at Greenspan the following morning. Another, almost miraculous, phone call, much like the one four years earlier, had come—this time from CNBC. I was one of two invited guests to respond to Greenspan on the morning CNBC news. I lived in Winter Haven, Florida at that time, so the closest TV station was in Tampa. I rushed over to the Tampa studio where I engaged in a three-way, debate-type short interview with the CNBC anchor in New York, and the other guest in Washington DC.

The adrenalin was really flowing by the time I got my chance to speak, and I held nothing back. I held a copy of my new book in front of the camera and said as forcefully as I could:

> Alan Greenspan should be ashamed of himself for what he is not telling the American people! It is the Bush tax cuts that are causing the problem!

It sure felt good to tell Greenspan off on that TV show. I felt certain that one of Greenspan's aides would make sure he viewed the video, given its nature. He would hear my angry words, and see the anger in my face.

But, by confronting Greenspan via TV, I probably drove the final nail into the coffin of my new book. Several weeks later, I would learn that *The Looting of Social Security* was no longer in bookstores, and Amazon.com would list the book as "unavailable."

I had emailed my editor on March 15, 2004 and asked how the book was selling. He responded with the following email.

Hi Allen,

"Your book is selling pretty well for us. We have shipped almost 8500 copies so far, with Barnes & Noble being the single largest customer for the book. They are averaging sales of around 60 copies per week chain wide. That's not a huge number, but it has been selling at that clip just about since they got copies last December. We have also just gone back to press for 1500 copies to replenish the stock that is moving through the system, which is good news." _____

I considered the email good news, and I thought the book was off to a good start. The first hint I got that there was a problem with availability came in a call from the organizer of a Social Security forum to be held at Shepherd University in Shepherdstown, West Virginia. I was scheduled to be co-speaker, along with James Roosevelt Jr. (FDR's grandson), and, as the forum neared, the organizer checked on the availability of my book in her area. I was astounded when she called and said,

> Your book is not available at any bookstore in the entire Baltimore–Washington, DC Metropolitan Area!

I was shocked. How could this be? I called bookstores around the country and verified that the book was no longer available. I sought the assistance of an employee at the Barnes & Noble bookstore in Naples, Florida to help me try to find out what had happened to the book. She checked the records for her store. She said they had received eight copies of the book initially. They had sold four copies when they were instructed, on May 10, 2004 to return the unsold books.

There were a lot of mysteries during that first year after "The Looting of Social Security" was published. As a

long-time member of the AARP, I just automatically
assumed that they would want to help expose the Social
Security fraud. In fact, I hoped they would review the book
in their publications and maybe even help to promote it. In
my mind, it was crucial to alert the public to the fact that
the Social Security money was being looted.

I sent copies of the book to the then CEO, William D.
Novelli, along with a letter seeking his help in exposing the
truth about the Social Security trust fund. I have in front of
me, as I write, Novelli's letter of response, dated April 9,
2004. It has been eleven years since I got that letter, and I
am still as dumbfounded by it as the day it arrived.

The AARP . chief scolded me for daring to expose the
looting of Social Security. He did not deny that the looting
was taking place, but he was adamant in his determination
to keep the public from finding out about the looting. He
wrote:

> To have a productive national debate about how to
> strengthen Social Security for future generations, it is vitally
> important that the American public has confidence in Social
> Security. Unfortunately, saying that the trust funds have
> been looted could result in people losing confidence in
> Social Security, and that is counterproductive.

Novelli made it very clear that he did not want to hear
from me again. He closed the letter by writing,

> If you want to discuss this issue further, please contact
> AARP 's Federal Affairs Department at @aarp.org.

I did try to get in touch with the contact person
Novelli referred me to, but without success. I tried to
contact various other AARP officials, by phone and by
email, but none of them would respond to me. It soon
became clear that I was persona non gratis at the AARP.

But I don't give up easily. I checked the list of new AARP board members who had been elected for the following year, and, to my delight, one of the new board members was a physician who practiced medicine in Orlando, just about 50 miles from where I live. I looked up the physician's contact information and sent an email to him through his private practice. I introduced myself and expressed my desire to discuss Social Security with someone from AARP.

The doctor responded to my email in a cordial manner and said he would do whatever he could to help me. He apologized for the behavior of fellow AARP officials and he seemed puzzled that nobody from the Washington Office would communicate with me. I asked him if he would read my book, if I mailed a copy to him. He said he would be happy to read it.

We exchanged emails for about three weeks, and he gave me useful feedback on the book. I soon began to envision him as my stepping stone into the hierarchy of the AARP And then it happened. I received the following email from the doctor.

"Dr. Smith,

I choose to have no further contact with you. May life be fair to both of us."

Dr. _____

I could hardly believe it. After numerous cordial email exchanges, why would the doctor end the correspondence this way? I emailed him several times, asking for an explanation. Finally, I suggested that I drive to Orlando and meet him for dinner at a restaurant of his choosing so we could have a private conversation. I waited and waited, and I hoped and hoped that he would get back in touch with me. But eleven years have now passed since that last short email exchange, and I have not heard another word from the good doctor from Orlando.

I am still somewhat haunted by the last sentence of the doctor's last email to me. "May life be fair to both of us." What did he mean by those strange words?

And that final message from the doctor in Orlando was also the final communication that I received from anyone at the AARP. I am still a member of the organization, and Joan and I use the AARP card to get a 20 percent discount off meals at Denny's every Saturday evening. But that is the full extent of my relationship with an organization that professes to want to save and protect Social Security.

Few people knew it at the time, but Federal Reserve Chairman, Alan Greenspan's February 25, 2004 call for Social Security benefit cuts was the opening salvo in an organized campaign to dismantle Social Security, as we now know it. On August 27, 2004, Greenspan again called for benefit cuts during remarks at a symposium in Jackson Hole, Wyoming.

Once George W. Bush was re-elected, Social Security reform suddenly rushed to the top of his domestic agenda. At a press conference on November 4, 2004, Bush said:

> Let me put it to you in this way. I earned capital in the campaign, political capital, and now I intend to spend it. It is my style...I'm going to spend it for what I told the people I'd spend it on, Social Security, tax reform, moving this economy forward.

At the time I lashed out at Greenspan, during my CNBC appearance in February 2004, the Bush Social Security privatization campaign was already in the early planning stages. The Bush people were probably scouting the road ahead to make sure there would be no surprises, or bumps in the road, that could derail the privatization campaign, once it got underway.

That 1100 word "review" of "The Looting of Social Security," which had appeared in the Washington Times in January, left little doubt as to what, at least one conservative—the reviewer—thought about me and the book. And it dramatically announced to the conservative world that someone was trying to expose the awful secret about the Social Security trust fund.

Even the possibility that my book might catch on and become widely read, would have been unacceptable to the Bush people. It would be a new "inconvenient truth" which would be just as unwelcome as Al Gore's "inconvenient truth" about global warming.

I don't know exactly what happened, but, some entity—a private individual, a conservative organization, an agency of government, or someone else—must have decided that "The Looting of Social Security" had to be rendered "unavailable" because it could wreck Bush's privatization campaign if it became widely read.

As soon as I was sure the book was definitely "unavailable," I contacted my publisher and requested that the publishing rights to the book be reverted back to me, so I could publish it elsewhere. But the publisher refused to relinquish the rights, which pretty much taped my mouth shut. Without owning the publication rights to the book, I couldn't even self-publish it.

When I vowed, in the year 2000, to continue my effort to expose the looting of Social Security money, for as long as it took, I gave little thought to how long it might take. Anyone could check the public record and verify, for themselves, that every dollar of the surplus Social Security revenue was being spent for non-Social Security purposes. All they had to do was to check the federal budget for the years after 1985, when the looting began.

But nobody had to resort to checking the federal budget numbers to know that Social Security money was being misused. The whole controversy blew up into a big news story when Senator Daniel Patrick Moynihan (D-NY) introduced legislation in 1990 to repeal the 1983 payroll tax hike and put Social Security back on a pay-as-you-go basis.

Senator Moynihan was outraged that, instead of being used to build up the Social Security trust fund for future retirees, the surplus Social Security revenue was being used to pay for general government spending. Moynihan, perhaps the best friend that Social Security ever had in Congress, believed the American people were being betrayed and cheated. His position was that, if the government couldn't keep its hands out of the Social Security cookie jar, he wanted the jar emptied so there would be no Social Security surplus to loot.

President Bush was furious over Moynihan's proposal. He had said in the campaign, "Read my lips-no new taxes." How could he keep that promise if his giant, secret Social Security slush fund was taken away?

Moynihan's proposal to repeal the 1983 payroll tax increase, and return Social Security to pay-as-you-go, had a lot of support from both conservatives and liberals. But President Bush used every resource at his command to defeat the Moynihan proposal.

It was another one of those things in life that would have changed so many other things if the vote had just gone the other way. Among other things, I would have been spared the need to devote fifteen years of my precious time on this earth to trying to expose the Social Security fraud. I don't know how I might have spent those years, if things had gone the other way. But, I'm pretty sure that whatever I might have done would have been a lot more fun than beating my head against a brick wall for fifteen years.

Getting back to Social Security, the truth about the trust fund sometimes gets some space on editorial pages, but reporting the story as part of the mainstream news is apparently still taboo. My wife, Joan, who has walked beside me every step of the way, throughout this fifteen-year odyssey, has a favorite question that she keeps on asking me.

"Allen," she asks.

"How do the news people know that they are not supposed to report the truth about Social Security?"

"Too many journalists still remember what happened to Dan Rather," I say.

"When Dan reported a story the White House didn't want reported, he got fired."

Why did Dan Rather have to go? He told a true story that embarrassed people in high places with lots of power. To this day, Rather is adamant that the only thing he was guilty of was telling the truth. In his new book, *Rather Outspoken: My Life in the News,* released in May 2012, Dan opens Chapter One with a strong defense of his past reporting. Below is short excerpt from that opening:

> Why was I out at CBS? Because I reported a true story. The story reported in September 2004 of President George W. Bush's dereliction of duty during Vietnam is true, and neither Bush himself nor anyone close to him—no family member, no confidante, no political ally—has ever denied it. I remain proud of reporting that truth, and proud of the many people who were part of the report.

Dan Rather, who is now 84 years old, is not the only victim of this injustice. The basic freedoms of expression in this great country have been damaged. Journalists cannot completely ignore what happened to Rather. Whether they are new to the profession or seasoned journalists in high places, the reality of their profession was changed by what happened to Dan Rather. Freedom of speech and freedom of the press are just a little less free than they once were.

The Social Security trust fund, alleged to have $2.7 trillion with which to pay benefits to the boomers, is empty. It holds no real assets of any kind. The only thing it has is a bunch of worthless government IOUs that can't be used to pay benefits, and couldn't be sold to anyone, even for a penny on the dollar. They are nothing more than pieces of paper that represent an accounting record of how much Social Security money has been spent on other programs.

On March 16, 2011, Senator Tom Coburn (R-OK) . dropped a bomb during a Senate speech that should have blasted sense into the heads of every one of his fellow members of Congress. But the bomb didn't explode like it should have.

Senator Coburn said, "Congresses under both Republican and Democrat control, both Republican and Democrat presidents, have stolen money from social security and spent it. The money's gone. It's been used for another purpose."

Every word that Senator Coburn spoke was absolutely true, and all members of Congress, and the President, know they are true. But the government doesn't want the public to know that the money is gone. And the mainstream media honors the government's wishes.

I hoped that Senator Coburn's admission that he and his fellow members of Congress had stolen money from Social Security and spent the money "for another purpose." would be widely reported by the news media. But very few people heard about the Senator's humble public confession.

Let's just focus on that remarkable fact, for a moment. Back in the 1970s and before, if a prominent United States Senator had publicly confessed that he and other members of Congress had stolen trillions of dollars from Social Security, "and used it for another purpose," that story would have been the lead story on the evening news. And, most of the nation's newspapers would have run headlines such as, "Senator Admits Stealing Social Security Money!" or "Social Security Trust Fund Robbed!"

But that did not happen on March 16, 2011, following Senator Coburn's statement. Instead, what most likely did happen is that Senator Coburn was probably severely chastised by both his colleagues and his party leaders for daring to say such a thing in public.

Our media today tells us what the government wants us to know, and very little more. It is built into the system. Journalist's careers depend upon them being able to interview public officials. And they do not want to be cut off from their sources by reporting something that was not supposed to have been reported.

Throughout my crusade to expose the Social Security fraud, I have written op-ed articles on the subject and submitted them to any news outlet that might publish them. Many of them were published by the internet newsletter, "Dissident Voice", a publication that refers to itself as "A radical newsletter in the struggle for peace and justice." But most of the mainstream media, including my local small-town newspaper, wouldn't touch my op-ed pieces.

CHAPTER TWO

SOCIAL SECURITY IS MORE VULNERABLE THAN YOU THINK

Some of my earliest memories from childhood are of my grandparents, and elderly neighbors, being excited about the new government program that many called "old-age pensions." It gave them a new safeguard against the uncertainties of growing old. Praise for Social Security was the only viewpoint I heard until I entered college. To the people I knew, Social Security was so popular that I didn't see how anyone could possibly be opposed to it.

But Social Security had harsh critics from the very beginning. The people who oppose Social Security do so, not because the program doesn't work, or because it is unpopular among the general public. On the contrary, Social Security is one of the most successful and popular programs ever created by the government.

Most opponents of Social Security are against it for ideological or political reasons. They don't believe the government should be trying to provide financial security to the elderly or to anyone else. They believe that the government should provide only for national defense, police protection and a few other things. These are the enemies of Social Security. These are the ones who have wanted to destroy the program ever since it was created in 1935. And they are closer to reaching their goal today than ever before.

Alf Landon, the Republican nominee for president in 1936, made the repeal of Social Security the main issue of his campaign. Landon said,

This is the largest tax bill in history. And to call it social security is a fraud on the workingman. I am not exaggerating the folly of this legislation. The Saving it forces on our workers is a cruel hoax.

Among other things, the 1936 election was a referendum on whether the American people wanted to keep or repeal Social Security. It was a massive victory for Roosevelt, who won the greatest electoral landslide since the beginning of the two-party system. He carried every state except Maine and Vermont. By winning 523 electoral votes, Roosevelt received more than 98 percent of the electoral vote. At the time, the election results seemed to settle the issue about the popularity of Social Security with the American people.

The enemies of Social Security did not go away, but they were almost invisible for decades. Over a period of many years, Social Security was known as the "third rail of politics," and most politicians were afraid to touch it. But that is no longer the case. A highly organized, and heavily funded, coalition of Social Security opponents has been working hard for the past 30 years to find a way to bring Social Security down. Dismantling Social Security is one of the highest priorities of conservatives.

Today, 78 years after Social Security was enacted in America, a lot of Social Security recipients tend to think of Social Security as an absolute American right that cannot be taken away, no matter what. And it should be. They pay into Social Security through the payroll tax and then, when they reach retirement age, the government will pay Social Security benefits to them for the rest of their lives. At least that is what most people who are currently drawing benefits seem to think. Nobody knows how long they will live, but Social Security recipients have always had confidence that their benefits would never be cut or taken away. For those who die before retirement age, benefits may be paid to eligible dependents. And those who become disabled before retirement age can apply for disability benefits. Throughout its 78-year history, the program has been popular, and most people have had great confidence in what they thought was the permanent and unchanging status of the program.

Did the action taken in 1983 make Social Security benefits a guaranteed right for all time? No. Social Security was created by Congress, and Congress has the authority to modify it, or even to end it. Section 1104 of the 1935 Social Security Act specifically states, "The right to alter, amend, or repeal any provision of this Act is hereby reserved to the Congress."

Section 1104 of the Social Security Act was not taken very seriously at first. It just didn't seem reasonable that the provision could be Constitutional. Americans were paying payroll taxes, which were dedicated exclusively to Social Security. So it didn't seem fair that Congress should have the authority to change or end the program. Most individuals, who were contributing to Social Security, seemed to believe that they would have an earned right to Social Security benefits, which could not be taken from them. But they were wrong.

In 1960, in the case of "Fleming v. Nestor," the United States Supreme Court, ruled that nobody has a "contractual earned right" to Social Security benefits. Specifically, the Supreme Court upheld the denial of benefits to Nestor, even though he had contributed to the program for 19 years and was already receiving benefits. In its ruling, the Supreme Court established the principle that entitlement to Social Security benefits "is not a contractual right."

This Court ruling was specific and without conditions. It made it legal for the government to deny benefits to people, no matter how much money they had contributed to the program. As long as Social Security was financially strong, and there was no organized movement to destroy it, the "Fleming v. Nestor" ruling was not very relevant. But the Court's decision is extremely relevant today. There is now a strong movement, by conservatives, to destroy Social Security, as we know it.

Social Security continues to be very popular with the American public. A CNN poll found that 80 percent of Americans think Social Security has been good for the country. With regard to age groups, it's not surprising that 90 percent of senior citizens believe Social Security has been good for the country, but it is a bit surprising that 70 percent of young adults feel the same way.

With so much public support, why wouldn't the government do whatever it has to do to keep Social Security safe and sound? In the 1950s, during the Eisenhower presidency, when the Republican party still put the interests of the nation above partisan politics, Social Security was not threatened. But the Republican Party has been increasingly taken over by a right-wing conservative movement, culminating in the formation of the Tea Party. These extreme conservatives want to create a very different America than we now have. They are on a mission to exterminate as many "New Deal" programs as possible, and Social Security is near the top of their list. They don't believe in such government programs, and they want to radically reduce taxes and the size of government.

Of all the possible threats to Social Security, the greatest threat is that enough of the anti-Social Security conservatives might gain enough political power to alter, or terminate the program. If Mitt Romney and Paul Ryan . had been elected President and Vice President, and the Republicans had gained control of the Senate, as well as the House, Social Security, as we now know it, would already be doomed. Privatization or other major structural changes to the program would be almost a certainty. The fact that the vast majority of Americans want to see Social Security continue in its present form would not have deterred

Romney and Ryan from going after the program. The Koch brothers and other wealthy conservative donors, would have succeeded in their dream of exterminating Social Security as if it were a poisonous snake.

Most Americans would have been shocked if the above scenario had actually taken place. Social Security had been only a minor issue in the campaign, and none of the candidates had publicly proposed exterminating it. But one of the most avid believers in getting rid of programs like Social Security (Paul Ryan) would have been just a heartbeat from becoming President of the United States, if the Republicans had won the election.

Ayn Rand, who was born and educated in Russia, before coming to the United States when she was 21 years old, was the founder of a radical philosophy known as Objectivism, or Randianism. She was an avowed atheist, whose beliefs were almost the exact opposite of traditional Judeo-Christian values. She argued that, "We are not our brothers' keepers." Instead, she believed that "Man's highest moral purpose in life is achievement of his own happiness." She said, "If any civilization is to survive, it is the morality of altruism that men have to reject. "

During an interview with Mike Wallace in 1959, Rand denounced government programs of all kinds. She said,

> "I feel that it is terrible that you see destruction all around you, and that you are moving toward disaster until and unless all those welfare state conceptions have been reversed and rejected. I am opposed to all forms of control. I am for an absolute, laissez-faire, free, unregulated economy."

Through her two famous novels, "Fountainhead" (1943) and "Atlas Shrugged" (1957), and her nonfiction book, "The Virtue of Selfishness" (1964), she has captured the hearts and minds of millions of Americans, including many in high places. Her best-known disciple, Alan Greenspan, was one of her associates for twenty years. Greenspan was so close to Rand that he invited her to stand beside him in the White House during his swearing-in ceremony to become President Ford's Chairman of the Council of Economic Advisors in 1974.

Actually, it was through a fellow associate of Ayn Rand that Greenspan got his first government job. Martin Anderson, also an associate of Ayn Rand, left the movement to join Nixon's first campaign. When Nixon won, he became Special Consultant to the President for Systems Analysis. It was through Anderson's recommendation that Alan Greenspan began his career in government. So, it was through Ayn Rand that Greenspan's many years of government service became a reality.

In his 2008 book, "The Age of Turbulence", Greenspan acknowledges just how much his thinking was influenced by Ayn Rand :

> " Ayn Rand became a stabilizing force in my life. It hadn't taken long for us to have a meeting of the minds—mostly my mind meeting hers—and in the fifties and early sixties I became a regular at the weekly gatherings at her apartment. She was a wholly original thinker, sharply analytical, strong-willed and highly principled. Exploring ideas with her was a remarkable course in logic and epistemology. Rand's collective became my first social circle outside the university and the economics profession. I engaged in the all-night debates and wrote spirited commentary for her newsletter with the fervor of a young acolyte drawn to a whole new set of ideas. Ayn Rand and I remained close until she died in 1982, and I'm

grateful for the influence she had on my life. I was intellectually limited until I met her."

Greenspan agrees that his 20-year association with Ayn Rand had an important influence on his thinking. He has said that Rand helped to wean him from an earlier liberalism and other "mistaken policies." If taken literally, his statement that he was intellectually limited before he met Ayn Rand, it appears that Greenspan believed that Rand had made him intellectually unlimited.

In the September 14, 1974 issue of "The New Republic," journalist Richard Strout reviews Greenspan's qualifications and background. Stroud begins the article with the following words. "I confess that Alan Greenspan startles me." He then goes on to explain why Greenspan startles him:

> What are his views? That is what is extraordinary. He opposes the antitrust law. He opposes the progressive income tax. He opposes consumer legislation as an interference with the free economy. He subscribes to a form of laissez-faire capitalism that has been elevated into a cult called objectivism. Its leader is controversial author philosopher, Ayn Rand, with a dogma that she terms "rational selfishness" (and that sounds like economic Darwinism.)

To make his point, Stroud quotes from some of Greenspan's earlier writings in Ayn Rand's periodical, "The Objectivist." Stroud reports that Greenspan wrote the following words in an article in July 1966:

> "The welfare state is nothing more than a mechanism by which governments confiscate the wealth of productive members of society to support a wide variety of welfare schemes."

According to Stroud, Greenspan defended the fact that Standard Oil controlled 80 percent of the oil refining capacity at the turn of the century, and argued that government should not have intervened. His justification of Standard Oil's monopoly power was explained as follows:

> Why not, he asked? Competition takes care of trusts if you leave them alone; this happens by a natural process for laissez-faire is the most efficient and productive of all possible economic systems.

Obviously, Greenspan's views were not consistent with the views of mainstream economists. If these views had become known prior to his Senate confirmation hearings, it seems highly unlikely that he would have been confirmed. As an economic adviser to President Ford, Greenspan gave bad advice. As Chairman of the Commission on Social Security Reform, Greenspan helped President Reagan push through an unwarranted payroll tax hike that ultimately led to $2.7 trillion of Social Security money being embezzled and spent for wars and other government programs. As Chairman of the Federal Reserve System, Greenspan played a major role in the 2008 financial meltdown and the Great Recession. Imagine how different things might have been if Mr. Greenspan had not gone to Washington.

As Rand stood beside Greenspan, during that swearing-in ceremony, she must have taken great satisfaction that her ideas and influence had finally made it all the way to the White House in the person of Alan Greenspan.

Greenspan was only one of many prominent Republicans who became fans of Ayn Rand and her writings. Supreme Court Justice Clarence Thomas. has such high regard for Rand's philosophy that each year he has his new law clerks come to his home and watch the

1949 film version of Ayn Rand's novel, *Fountainhead*. Rand's writings apparently played a key role in Clarence Thomas's conversion from left-wing radicalism to conservatism. In his book, "My Grandfather's Son," Clarence Thomas writes:

> Rand preached a philosophy of radical individualism that she called Objectivism. While I didn't fully accept its tenets, her vision of the world made more sense to me than that of my left-wing friends. What I wanted was for everyone—the government, the racists, the activists, the students, even Daddy—to leave me alone so that I could finally start thinking for myself.

The 2012 Republican Vice Presidential nominee, Paul Ryan, is such a strong admirer of Ayn Rand that he makes "Atlas Shrugged" required reading for all his interns and staff, and has given out copies of the book as Christmas presents.

In a 2005 speech that Paul Ryan gave to the Atlas Society, a group of Ayn Rand devotees, Ryan revealed a great deal about his thinking and how he wants to change Social Security, Ryan said:

> "I grew up reading Ayn Rand, and it taught me quite a bit about who I am and what my value systems are, and what my beliefs are. It's inspired me so much that it's required reading in my office for all my interns and my staff.
>
> In almost every fight we are involved in here, it is a fight that usually comes down to one conflict: individualism vs. collectivism that is why there is no more fight that is more obvious between the differences of these two conflicts than Social Security. Social Security right now is a collectivist system, it's a welfare transfer system.
>
> If we do not succeed in switching these programs, in reforming these programs from what some people call a defined benefit system, to a defined contribution system–

from switching these programs—and this is where I'm talking about health care, as well from a third party or socialist based system to an individually owned, individually pre-funded, individually directed system."

Other prominent people who have expressed admiration for Ayan Rand and her ideas include: Ronald Reagan, John Boehner, Senator Ron Johnson. Ron Paul, Senator Rand Paul, Rush Limbaugh, Glen Beck, Sean Hannity, Newt Gingrich, Eric Cantor, Mitch McConnell, and many others.

Ayn Rand died in 1982, but the movement, based on her philosophy, is even stronger today than when she was alive, and it is picking up steam. Ayn Rand's 1964 book entitled, *The Virtue of Selfishness,* sold 400,000 copies during the first four months after publication. Half a century later, in 2013, it is still selling at a hefty pace. In 2011, *Atlas Shrugged* sold 445,000 copies, the second strongest sales year in the novel's 54-year history.

I believe this movement to radically change the face of America is a great threat to Social Security as we now know it. The followers of Rand are not opposed to Social Security because it doesn't work, or isn't popular with the public. In their eyes, the very existence of Social Security is an evil that must be exterminated. They see it as a cancer on the face of America that must be eradicated in order to make America whole.

As I write these words, it seems like a bad nightmare that will be gone when I awaken. But it won't be gone for a very long time, because the movement is becoming stronger and stronger. The fact that one of the most dedicated followers of Ayn Rand's radical philosophy served as chairman of the Federal Reserve System for nearly two decades, is frightening. But, even more scary, is the fact that a person with these radical beliefs (Paul Ryan) almost came within a heartbeat of becoming President of the United States.

This movement has become very strong at a time when most Americans don't have a clue as to what the beliefs and goals of these conservatives are. They were key players in the irresponsible behavior that led to the first downgrade in America's credit rating in history. They are responsible for the gridlock in Congress. They believe that obstructing progress is more important than compromising their beliefs.

The fact that Ayn Rand is an atheist, who was born and educated in Russia, does not bother me nearly as much as the radical ideas and philosophy of her movement. Her followers are trying to turn America into a very different country than it has ever been before. They are engaging in class warfare against the middle and lower classes in an effort to give still more power and wealth to the very rich. Beware of wolves in sheep's clothing. The vision that the Randians have in mind for this country is not at all what they are portraying to the public, and it is certainly not what our founding fathers had in mind.

A small hint of the thinking of today's conservatives slipped out when Romney categorized "47 percent." of Americans as "different" from the rest of the population. Paul Ryan calls these people "takers" who take from the people who are "makers." And Ayn Rand calls the "inferior" people "moochers," "looters," and "parasites" who take from the "producers."

Ayn Rand goes even farther. She holds nothing but disdain for people who try to serve others. She said:

> The man who attempts to live for others is a dependent. He is a parasite in motive and makes parasites of those he serves. The relationship produces nothing but mutual corruption. It is impossible in concept. The nearest approach to it in reality – the man who lives to serve others – is the slave. If physical slavery is repulsive, how much more repulsive is the concept of servility of the spirit. The conquered slave has a vestige of honor. He has the merit of having resisted and of considering his condition evil. But the

man who enslaves himself voluntarily in the name of love is the basest of creatures. He degrades the dignity of man, and he degrades the conception of love. But that is the essence of altruism. "

The extremist in the Republican party have great admiration for Ayn Rand and her notion that selfishness is a virtue and helping others is a vice to be avoided. I don't believe that any of our founding fathers would have endorsed such a philosophy. This is not Americanism. This is the antitheses of Americanism.

It is the relentless organized political movement to get rid of Social Security, as we now know it, that is the greatest threat to Social Security. America dodged a bullet in the 2012 election, but we might not be so lucky in 2016. We may end up with someone who is even more extreme in their determination to privatize Social Security. Make no mistake about it. The conservative wing of the Republican party has declared war on Social Security.

The assumptions underlying Objectivism are severely flawed and unworkable. It is based on what they call totally free, uncontrolled laissez-faire capitalism. There is no such thing, except in the distorted minds of those who advocate it. The phrase laissez-faire is French and literally means "let do" or "let it be." Proponents of such a system advocate getting rid of most government regulations, radically reducing taxes and allowing big business to do whatever it wants to do. (We saw what happened when Wall Street was deregulated.)

Such an economic system has never existed and would certainly not be workable in today's world. Almost all major economies in the world are mixed economies in that both markets and some government participation are involved in making basic economic decisions. The United States economy is predominantly a market economy with most economic decisions being made by a system of free markets. Those who allege that the United States is moving toward socialism don't know what socialism, as an economic system, really is.

Socialism is usually defined as an economic system under which the government owns and operates the means of production. Capitalism is usually defined as an economic system based on private ownership and operation of the means of production for profit.

It is important to recognize that socialism and capitalism are economic systems—not political systems. Communist countries like China and Cuba combine the economic system of socialism with the political system of Communism. However, Sweden and numerous other countries, combine socialism with democracy.

Sweden is a very successful nation. Like the United Kingdom, it is a constitutional monarchy with a parliamentary democracy form of government. Sweden has the world's eighth highest per capita income. In 2010, the World Economic Forum ranked Sweden as the second most competitive country in the world, after Switzerland.

Conservatives who claim that the United States is headed toward ruin because it has a few government social programs never point to Sweden as an example of socialism. They make comparisons with Communist countries like Cuba who combine the economic system of socialism with the communist political system. Socialism is the economic system favored by the majority of voters in Sweden, and it works well for them, just as capitalism works well for the United States of America.

The United States is in no way a socialist economy. It never has been, and it probably never will be. The United States is a market economy with private ownership of most of the means of production. However, even in a market economy, there is a need for the government to make sure that people play by the rules, and there are some things, which the government can do more efficiently than private enterprise. I believe that Social Security is one of those things that the government can do for the people better than private enterprise.

Abraham Lincoln said: "The government should do for the people only those things which the people cannot do for themselves, or cannot do as well for themselves." That is the exact criteria that I subscribe to. For example, President Kennedy believed, and Congress agreed, that the United States should set a goal of sending man to the moon and bringing him back safely within a decade. There were various reasons for doing so, including national security concerns and America's status in the fields of science and technology, as viewed by the rest of the world.

Why didn't the private sector fulfill this need? The private sector would not have found the moon launch profitable. The major goal of private enterprise, as it should be, is to earn a profit. If the costs of an undertaking will be greater than the revenue earned, it doesn't make sense for private enterprise to do it. The only way that man would be sent to the moon and returned to earth safely was for the government to do it. Therefore, the race to the moon was a proper role for the government. National defense and police protection are other areas where government needs to be involved.

Early in American history, there was a dire need for a national postal system, but private investors would not have been able or willing to build such a system. So, the government had to do it. Today, FedEx, UPS, and a number of other private carriers are competing very successfully with the United States Post Office.

Adam Smith in his monumental book, "The Wealth of Nations," published in 1776, described a hypothetical economy, different from any economy that has ever existed. He specified the circumstances that would have to exist, such as no monopoly power, enough competition to prevent any party from taking advantage of another party, no patents, no labor unions and numerous other conditions, that would have to exist for a totally free-market economy to work.   He then explains that, in such a hypothetical economy, unregulated capitalism might work in such a way that, when individuals sought their own self- interest, the common good would prevail.

Adam Smith was describing a hypothetical economy that was very different from any economic system that has ever existed anywhere in the world. The American economy is very different from Adam Smith's hypothetical economy.   Some sectors of the American economy come close to working the way Adam Smith's hypothetical economy was supposed to work. But, other sectors are very different from the economy Smith described.

For example, the fast food industry has so much competition that they must provide a good product at a fair price in order to keep their customers.   In many communities, there will be a McDonald's, a Burger King, a Wendy's, and possibly several other fast food outlets all within a few blocks of each other. If any of the restaurants charge more that the average price for the community, their sales will plummet. Similarly, if the quality of the product of any given restaurant should deteriorate, consumers will abandon that restaurant and take their business to competitors. Thus, in the case of the fast food industry, competition is sufficient to prevent buyers and sellers from taking advantage of each other.

If the entire economy were organized like the fast food industry, there would be no need for the government to intervene.   But most of the major industries are oligopolies or monopolies.   By gaining control of raw materials, or having patent protection on a product, companies can avoid competition and take advantage of customers through excessive prices or poor quality of the product.

The pharmaceutical industry is a good example of why the government has to partially regulate some industries. Suppose one of the major pharmaceutical companies were to develop a new drug, which millions of people must have in order to stay alive. The patent laws would allow the company to avoid competition for many years. The company would be looking out for its best interests by charging the highest possible price for the drug. Rich people could buy the drug, but many poor people would not have access to the life-sustaining drug. Such a situation might be good for the self-interest of the company, but it would certainly not be good for the population as a whole.

This is a case where the government might require the owner of the patent to sell production rights to other companies so the drug could be mass-produced and sold at a price that most people could afford. This is an example of why the economy cannot be allowed to operate freely without any government regulations.

The question that needs to be answered is, "How much regulation?" Not whether or not there should be any government regulation. Private enterprise is alive and well in the United States of America. Paul Ryan and other right-wing politicians know this fact well. But they are willing to lie to the American people, and use scare tactics, as part of their drive to destroy Social Security. Social Security has existed and flourished since 1935. It remained strong during the McCarthy era of the early 1950s, when crazy men were calling almost everyone, including President Eisenhower, Communists.

Why should America today allow a bunch of liars, to destroy Social Security, just because Ayn Rand didn't like it? The right-wing politicians hate Social Security, Medicare, and other similar programs. They show no respect for the millions of Americans who like Social Security and have always counted on it to be there. How dare Paul Ryan lead a movement to destroy Social Security when he is one of very few of the younger members of

Congress who has actually received and spent Social Security benefit money?

Because of the early death of his father, Ryan drew Social Security survivors' benefits from age 16 to age 18, which enabled him to build up a nest egg fund to help him pay for college. No one should begrudge Ryan for accepting benefits, which he was entitled to. But how could he be so callous as to try to drastically cut Social Security benefits so that future, equally-deserving Social Security beneficiaries would be unable to finance a college education from the same source that had benefited him so much?

Ayn Rand and her followers ignore American history with regard to what happens without government regulation. The following paragraph from the Federal Trade Commission (FTC) describes the state of the economy before enactment of the anti-trust laws.

> Once upon a time, way back in the 1800s, there were several giant businesses known as "trusts." They controlled whole sections of the economy, like railroads, oil, steel, and sugar. Two of the most famous trusts were U.S. Steel and Standard Oil; they were monopolies that controlled the supply of their product—as well as the price. With one company controlling an entire industry, there was no competition, and smaller businesses and people had no choices about from whom to buy. Prices went through the roof, and quality didn't have to be a priority. This caused hardship and threatened the new American prosperity.

John D. Rockefeller was one of the most notorious and ruthless titans who refused to play by any set of ethical rules and took advantage of his competitors. His company, Standard Oil, owned 20,000 domestic wells, 4,000 miles of pipeline, 5,000 tank cars, and had over 100,000 employees. Standard Oil's share of world oil refining topped out above 90 percent. Rockefeller had a bag of dirty tricks which destroyed his competitors. He bought out most smaller oil companies at bargain basement prices. Those who refused to bend were broken to bits like tiny twigs before he took them over. Rockefeller bought up railroads and pipelines that transported oil from the wells to the market. Once he controlled the supply lines, he refused to transport the oil of the hold-out companies, forcing them into bankruptcy where he could buy them for pennies on the dollar of their original value.

That is an example of what happens with unrestrained free market capitalism. Ayn Rand apparently never studied basic economics. Because, if she had, she would have recognized the importance of competition in a market economy. Free market capitalism cannot work without strong competition, and some central authority to make sure the market remains competitive. That is why the antitrust laws were enacted, and why the antitrust division of the Justice Department was created.

When Ronald Reagan became President in 1981, one of his favorite statements was "Government is not the solution. Government is the problem." He pushed for rolling back regulations that had been in effect for decades. That policy was continued for four more years under George H.W. Bush, and eight more years under George W. Bush, and it ultimately culminated with the 2008 Financial Meltdown and the Great Recession. For 20 of the 28 years, between 1981 and 2008, conservative Republican policies, like the ones advocated by Ayn Rand and her disciples, were in effect and they led to the greatest calamity to our economy since the Great Depression.

Still, conservativess are trying to force the country into returning to those tragic days and ending, or privatizing, Social Security is one of their first goals. If enough Republicans get elected to turn this goal into reality, Social Security is doomed.

As pointed out earlier in this chapter, Congress and the President have the legal authority to change, or even terminate, Social Security. And the 1960 United States Supreme Court decision, "Fleming v. Nestor," leaves beneficiaries with no legal recourse.

Social Security could easily be put back on a sustainable track, if the government would make arrangements for gradually repaying the $2.7 trillion that it has stolen from the Social Security fund.

The money could be repaid in installments over a period of years as more and more of the baby boomers retire. But politicians will do so only if there is an unprecedented effort to pressure members of Congress to repay the money. If the majority of the baby boomers joined in a national public outcry, demanding that the stolen Social Security money be repaid, I think it would be repaid. The bottom line is that the future of Social Security is really in the hands of the American public.

CHAPTER THREE

ECONOMIC ILLITERACY
AND MALPRACTICE

During my four years in graduate school at Indiana University, it didn't even occur to me that we might be a nation of economic illiterates. My professors and fellow students were all very proficient in economics, so it was only after I completed my Ph.D. and went out into the real world that I became aware of just how little the general public knows about economics. And it wasn't just those people who hadn't attended college. It included doctors and lawyers, and the vast majority of my fellow faculty members (outside the economics department) at the state university where I taught.

I just didn't realize that it was possible for a person to become a medical doctor, a lawyer, a college professor, or even a member of Congress, without having ever been exposed to basic economics. But that is indeed the sorry state that we find ourselves in, even today. Some of the most educated people in this nation are economically illiterate, including the vast majority of members of Congress. That is a major problem for America, and it helps to explain the ridiculously incompetent economic policies that have often been in effect.

Economic illiteracy made possible the terrible economic malpractice by the government over a period of three decades. Economic malpractice is to economics what medical malpractice is to medicine. When the government ignores mainstream economists, and implements programs that the majority of mainstream economists oppose, it is practicing economic malpractice.

Beginning with President Reagan in 1981, our government turned its back on the traditional economic policies, under which the economy had operated for the previous 40 years, and implemented a new untested theory called "supply-side economics," which soon became commonly called "Reaganomics." That was the beginning of the journey toward the 2008 Financial Meltdown and the accompanying Great Recession. These policies severely damaged our economy and caused massive needless suffering.

Millions of Americans have lost their homes to foreclosure, tens of millions have lost their jobs, families have broken apart and desperate individuals, who lost all hope, have committed suicide. None of these things needed to happen. They were not the result of natural forces, which were beyond the control of mankind. On the contrary, they were the result of deliberate actions by the government as part of a long-range political plan to reduce taxes and dramatically reduce the size of government.

None of these irresponsible government actions would have been possible if the majority of Americans had a basic understanding of how the economy works. Voters would not have elected candidates whose proposals were the exact opposite of what the majority of professional economists advocated. The economic policies for 20 of the 28 years between 1981 and 2009 were driven, not by what is good for the economy, but by the political objectives of extreme conservatives who want to turn our country into something that it has never been and was never intended to be. They were pursuing a hidden agenda to reduce government revenue to such a point that the government would be forced to make radical cuts in programs, which they never could have done through the open democratic process.

Because most Americans have no formal education in economics, they have little knowledge of how the American economy operates. Yet, these economically illiterate people determine the official economic policies of the nation by casting their votes for President and for members of Congress. And there is often a basic contradiction between what is politically popular, and what is best for the economy. For example, tax cuts are always popular with taxpayers. But proper management of the economy requires tax cuts at certain times and tax increases at other times.

No matter what the circumstances of the economy call for, conservatives usually propose cutting taxes, even though it might be the worst possible policy for the economy. The hidden agenda of the conservatives has always been their desire to "starve the beast." Their goal has been to reduce revenue to the point where the government is forced to cut popular and much-needed programs.

If most Americans had been even moderately literate in economics they would never have elected Ronald Reagan President. They would have seen how Reagan's promised massive tax cuts would lead to economic disaster. And, even though they would have liked the big tax cuts, they would rather have sound economic policies that would keep the economy strong for the future. But the American people were so economically illiterate that they bought a pig in a poke. They trusted Ronald Reagan to be honest with them about the consequences of the massive tax cuts. If Reagan said the tax cuts would be good for the economy, most Americans believed him and ignored what others were saying.

None of us would entrust the maintenance and repair of our automobiles to anyone except highly-skilled and well-trained auto technicians. If we are so particular about who does the maintenance on our automobile, why wouldn't we insist that the far-more-complex mechanism called the American economy also be maintained and repaired at least under the guidance of highly-trained experts?

High school students are required to study American History and American Government, presumably so they will be "better citizens" and "better-informed" voters. This is good, but it is impossible to have a clear understanding of either United States History or American Government without a clear understanding of basic economic principles and a knowledge of how the American Economy operates.

My children attended the local school system in the university town where I taught, and it appeared to be a high-quality school district in most respects. But I was absolutely shocked when my son entered high school and discovered that the school did not even teach economics. In my opinion, every high school should teach economics and require students to take the course as a graduation requirement. For a school to not even offer an elective course in economics, for those students who wanted to study economics, is almost unbelievable. I asked one of the high school history teachers why they didn't offer an economics course. His reply was, "None of the teachers want to teach it."

Only 22 states require high school students to take a course in economics before graduation. That being the case, I firmly believe that it should become a top priority of every high school in America to add a course in economics to their curriculum, if they don't already have one. Also, I don't understand how any college can consider its students fully educated without students being required to take an economics course.

Whenever I bring up the need for universal economics education with non-economists, their response is always the same. "You can't require economics without requiring chemistry, physics, and other important courses. Why single out economics as a course for special treatment?"

The answer is that, unlike chemistry and physics, individuals have to make decisions every day of their lives that involve economics. And every time people vote, they have to decide which candidates are advocating sound economic policies. The fact that some students haven't had a course in chemistry is not a threat to our economy. Lack of education in economics is.

When Congress passes legislation involving chemistry, they will call on chemistry experts to guide them, because members of Congress know that most of them are not literate in chemistry. By contrast, when Congress enacted Reagan's radical "supply-side" proposals in 1981, government officials ignored the advice of most mainstream economists and allowed politicians to formulate economic policy. Most of these politicians were just as illiterate in economics as they were in chemistry. The difference is that they know they are illiterate in chemistry, but don't realize that they are equally illiterate in economics.

The year, 1981, represented a radical turning point for the American economy. The United States government abandoned most of the proven economic policies that had guided the economy for the previous four decades. Economists were cast aside, and radical political policies, masquerading as economic policies, were put into effect. The economy was put on a track that would ultimately lead to disaster for this country and the rest of the world. The Financial Meltdown of 2008 and the accompanying severe recession were the ultimate outcome of these policies. The 12 years of economic policies under Reagan and George H.W. Bush pushed the economy almost to the brink of disaster.

Fortunately, when Bill Clinton became President in 1992, he returned the nation to sound economic policies, based on the same traditional economic theory that had dominated American economic policy for more than 40 years prior to the election of President Reagan. Clinton gradually brought the budget deficits down and actually had budget surpluses during his last two years in office—

the first budget surpluses in 38 years. Clinton had repaired much of the damage done to the economy by Reagan and George H.W. Bush. Both the budget and the economy were in good shape when Clinton turned the reins of power over to George W. Bush on January 20, 2001. There were still problems, but Clinton had pulled the economy back from the brink of disaster, and he had put it on a sustainable track forward.

As future historians look back at the transition from the 20th century to the 21st century, and the November 2000 Presidential election, they will scratch their heads in disbelief. They will compare the economic records of the 12 years under Reaganomics with the 8 years of traditional economic policies under President Clinton. The failure of Reaganomics, and the success of traditional economics under Clinton, will be so clear to them that they may conclude that the American people must have suffered from some kind of mass insanity in the fall of 2000. How else will they explain why the American people put George W. Bush in the White House, knowing that he would return the economy to the same policies that had failed so miserably under both Reagan and Bush's father?

America was given a second chance when Clinton was elected President. He put the economy back on track and eliminated the deficit. But George W. Bush managed to push the economy back to the brink, and then push it over the edge, before his second term came to an end. He had inherited such a prosperous and sound economy from Clinton, but, in less than eight years, Bush managed to plunge the American economy into the most severe economic crisis since the Great Depression of the 1930s. As a result, Bush's successor inherited a set of circumstances worse than that of any previous president except Lincoln. The economy was plunging downward, and out of control, when Barack Obama began his presidency.

Even before the Reagan administration had implemented any of its voodoo economic policies, Americans were warned of the dangers inherent in Reagan's proposals. Paul Samuelson, the first American to receive the coveted Nobel prize in economics, was shouting out warnings from the rooftops. Samuelson, who wrote a regular column for *Newsweek* at the time, had access to a mass audience, and he did everything in his power to alert the public to the inherent dangers in Reagan's economic proposals. Below is an excerpt from an article by Samuelson that appeared in the March 2, 1981 issue of "Newsweek."

> "Reagan's program does attempt a radical break with the past. A radical-right crusade is being sold as a solution for an economy allegedly in crisis. There is no such crisis! Our people should join this crusade only if they agree with its philosophical conservative merits. They should not be flim-flammed by implausible promises that programs to restore the 1920s' inequalities will cure the inflation problem."

It was like shouting into the wind for Dr. Samuelson. Very few Americans cared about what professional economists thought, even Nobel prize-winning economists. They believed whatever the charismatic Reagan told them. He had promised that he could deliver a major tax cut and still balance the budget by 1984. Why should the people take the word of Samuelson over that of the President who had just been elected by a landslide? Never mind that Reagan chose a 34-year-old, with no training in economics, as the chief architect of his economic policy, or that he ignored the advice of his own Council of Economic Advisers. Surely the President knew what he was doing.

Although his policies inflicted great damage upon the American economy, Reagan continued to say throughout his presidency, "The American economy has never been healthier or stronger." Instead of acknowledging that Reaganomics had led to catastrophic deficits and a skyrocketing national debt, and taking remedial actions, Reagan continued to stubbornly insist that his economic policies were sound, despite the abundant evidence to the contrary. And the most disturbing part of it all is that the American people continued to believe him.

Ronald Reagan got to the White House primarily because he promised large tax cuts that the nation could not afford. The consequences of these policies put the economy on the road to economic collapse. During his first six years as President, Ronald Reagan added as much to the national debt as all previous presidents combined, from George Washington through Jimmy Carter had added in more than 200 years. And that was just the beginning of our problems. The problem has been that the government used politicians—not economists—to determine economic policies for the nation.

The "great communicator" was capable of charming the people into believing the economy was strong and healthy. However, when George H.W. Bush tried to follow in Reagan's footsteps, he was unable to convince Americans that the economy was in good shape. Although President Bush seemed such a sure bet for re-election in 1992 that most of the top contenders for the Democratic nomination chose not to run, Bill Clinton saw the incumbent president as vulnerable because of the state of the economy and the negative effects of Reaganomics.

Economics is one of the six categories in which the coveted Nobel prize is awarded to persons "who have made outstanding contributions for the benefit of mankind." The other five categories are, medicine, physics, chemistry, literature, and peace.

During the Reagan administration, budget Director David Stockman, who had never had even an introductory course in the field of economics, became one of the chief architects of economic policy and totally ignored and defied the warnings of outstanding professional economists' some of whom had been awarded the Nobel Prize.

America paid an enormous price for that economic malpractice. Yet, in the 2000 presidential election, the American people elected a new president who was expounding proposals, including a major tax cut, that were totally contrary to the thinking of most mainstream professional economists. Most Americans, including top government officials, do not know much more about economics than they know about chemistry or physics. However, they are aware that they don't know much about chemistry or physics, but unaware that they are equally illiterate in the field of economics.

Probably the first time that any administration was guilty of economic malpractice was during the Great Depression. However, it is hard to hold Hoover responsible because modern economic science was still in its infancy. And, although Roosevelt was slow to take the correct actions, he did gradually implement fairly sound economic policies.

The Employment Act of 1946 requires the President to appoint a Council of Economic Advisors to the President. The purpose of this requirement was to make sure that the President always had close access to some of the top economists in the nation. The problem is that some past presidents have totally ignored the advice of their own economic advisers and deliberately engaged in economic malpractice.

President Lyndon B. Johnson was the first president to flagrantly violate the intent of the Employment Act of 1946 by turning his back on the sound economic advice of his economic advisers and listening instead to his political advisers. Johnson's economic advisers urged him to raise taxes to offset the substantial increase in military expenditures on the Vietnam War. They warned that failure to do so could set off a prolonged period of high inflation. However, Johnson's political advisers told him that to do so would not be good politics. They suggested that to tell the American people that they were going to have to pay more taxes because of the war would be the equivalent of political suicide. At this time, the war was becoming increasingly unpopular with the people, so they would be especially irritated at the prospects of paying higher taxes for the war. Johnson believed that raising taxes would prevent him from being elected to another term, and so he placed personal political considerations above pursuing sound economic policies.

America paid an incredible price for President Johnson's failure to listen to the advice of his own hand-picked Council of Economic Advisers. In 1965, the economy was in one of the best positions ever. The unemployment rate was 4.5 percent, the inflation rate was 1.6 percent, and the government ran a budget deficit of only $1.4 billion. This was the seventh year in a row that the inflation rate had remained below 2 percent, and the unemployment rate was at its lowest level in 8 years. The federal budget was almost in balance, and the nation exported more goods than it imported. And then we blew it!

The escalation of the Vietnam War in 1966 led to a substantial unplanned increase in military expenditures. The large increase in government spending caused total spending to rise above the full-employment capacity of the economy. With total spending exceeding the capacity of the economy to produce, prices began to rise and the nation embarked on a long journey of demand-pull inflation.

After seven years with inflation rates below two percent, the inflation rate rose to 2.9 percent in 1966, 4.2 percent in 1968, and 5.5 percent in 1969. The inflation was to get much worse during the 1970s and 1980s—11.0

percent in 1974, and 13.5 percent in 1980. Although much of the inflation of the 1970s resulted from the energy crises and soaring prices for crude oil, these special problems just added to the inflationary pressures started in the 1960s when the government failed to raise taxes in time to prevent the increased spending on the Vietnam War from setting off a prolonged period of demand-pull inflation. It took sixteen years and the most severe economic downturn since the Great Depression (the 1981-82 recession) to break the back of the inflationary pressures set off by the economic malpractice during the Johnson years.

President Lyndon Johnson ignored the advice of his own economic advisers in order to pursue political goals. The cost of this unforgivable economic malpractice was enormous. Millions of Americans suffered needlessly because of the failure of the president to follow sound economic advice.

Johnson may have been the first president to deliberately engage in economic malpractice, but he would certainly not be the last one. As you will see in the following chapters, Ronald Reagan, H.W. Bush and George W. Bush abandoned traditional economic policies and experimented with the economy. They ignored the advice of their own economic advisors, as well as that of the top economists in the country. They concentrated on achieving major political objectives, such as reducing taxes and the size of government, while allowing the economy to deteriorate to the breaking point of the 2008 financial meltdown and the accompanying Great Recession.

The specific details of the economic malpractice will be explained in the following chapters. However, before leaving this chapter, I want to present an overview of the negative economic policies, and their consequences, during the presidencies of Ronald Reagan, George H.W. Bush, and George W. Bush.

There was never any attempt to follow the traditional economic policies that had been followed successfully for 40 years prior to Reagan's presidency. The Reagan Revolution was not about sound economics. It was about permanently changing America—both the government and the economy—into a system of small government and low taxes.

As we discussed in the previous chapter, Ayn Rand was a Russian-born and educated writer who came to the United States when she was 21 years old. She is famous for her two novels, "Fountainhead" and "Atlas Shrugged," and also for her nonfiction book, "The Virtue of Selfishness." She considered altruism an idea that people must reject in order to be successful. She argued that man's only purpose is to maximize his own happiness, and she rejected the idea that "We are our brothers' keepers."

Rand advocated a theoretical system, called laissez-faire capitalism, under which there would be little or no government regulation, and the government would provide for national defense, police protection, and only a few more things. A free-market system would replace the role of government regulation. The size of the federal government, and the role it plays in the economy, would be radically reduced enabling major tax cuts.

Ronald Reagan, George H.W. Bush, and George W. Bush focused on reducing revenue so severely that the government would be forced to greatly reduce the size of government. That is what the Reagan Revolution and the Tea Party movement are all about. And, in terms of its political goals, the conservative movement has made a lot of progress. Alan Greenspan was a close associate to Ayn Rand for more the 20 years, and he credits her with inspiring his thinking. Paul Ryan has said that he grew up reading Ayn Rand, and he gives her credit for his decision to enter government service. Ryan also makes Rand's novel required reading for his staff and has given out copies of the book as Christmas presents. Given the fact that Ayn Rand is an avowed atheist, her books might not be appreciated by some as a Christmas gift.

Today's conservatives divide the American people into two categories—makers and takers. Ayn Rand used harsher terms. She called the takers moochers, looters and parasites. These are the people Romney referred to as the 47 percent. Believers in this philosophy look at lower-income Americans with disdain, and contend that it is wrong to help such people. To put it in a nutshell, they think that the rich should get richer as the poor become poorer. They do not believe the government should collect taxes from the rich and use those tax dollars to help the poor.

The struggle is between the "haves" and "have nots." When anyone complains about the big gap between rich and poor, they are silenced by the "haves" with accusations that the "have nots" are engaging in class warfare. Class warfare has been going on since the beginning of time, and the rich are almost always the winners. As a result of Reaganomics, income and wealth have been substantially redistributed, from the poor and middle class, to the rich.

Over the past 30 years, the rich have become richer and the poor have become poorer. We have been living in a Robin Hood-in-reverse society. Instead of taking from the rich in order to help the poor and disadvantaged, we have been taking from the poor in order to make the rich even richer. Former Secretary of Labor, Robert Reich, who is a labor economist, shows the reverse income distribution in his book, *Beyond Outrage*. Reich compares the share the nation's total income going to the highest income Americans during the 1960s and 1970s with the share going to the rich in 2007.

According to Reich, during the 1960s and 1970s, the wealthiest 1 percent of families received 9-10 percent of the total income. By 2007, the share going to the top 1 percent was 23.5 percent. Thus, the share of income going to the top 1 percent more than doubled during the period. If we look at the very top, the one-tenth of one percent, we find that their share of income tripled.

Undoubtedly, the massive tax cuts under Reagan, and again under George W. Bush, played a major role in this income distribution reversal. Although almost everyone got a tax cut, the cuts went disproportionately to the wealthiest Americans. There was a lot of income inequality even before Reagan made his first big tax cuts. But there is a lot more inequality today than when Reaganomics was launched.

CHAPTER FOUR

HOW IT ALL STARTED

Ronald Reagan was one of the most popular presidents in modern history. As a former Hollywood actor, he had an uncommon degree of charisma. The conservatives absolutely loved Reagan for his efforts to reduce the size of government, but most liberals hated him with a passion. Reagan is still revered by a lot of Americans. This reverence for Ronald Reagan helps to explain how he was able to fool most of the American people to a degree unparalleled by any other modern president. With the help of Alan Greenspan, Reagan pulled off one of the greatest frauds ever perpetrated against the American people.

It is so ironic that many people, today, still believe that Ronald Reagan came galloping up on a great white horse to sound the alarm that Social Security was in deep financial trouble. He then allegedly figured out a solution to the problem and rammed his legislative proposal through Congress in a three-month period. On April 20, 1983, the signing ceremony for the new legislation took place with great fanfare. Below are some of Reagan's remarks at the signing ceremony.

> This bill demonstrates for all time our nation's ironclad commitment to social security. It assures the elderly that America will always keep the promises made in troubled times a half a century ago. It assures those who are still working that they, too, have a pact with the future. From this day forward, they have our pledge that they will get their fair share of benefits when they retire. Today, all of us can look each other square in the eye and say, "We kept our promises." We promised that we would protect the financial integrity of social security. We have. We promised that we would protect beneficiaries against any loss in current benefits. We have. And we promised to attend to the needs

of those still working, not only those Americans nearing
retirement but young people just entering the labor force.
And we've done that, too

Instead of being a proud day for America, April 20,
1983, has become a day of shame. The Social Security
Amendments of 1983 laid the foundation for 30-years of
federal embezzlement of Social Security money in order to use
the money to pay for wars, tax cuts and other government
programs. The payroll tax hike of 1983 generated a total of
$2.7 trillion in surplus Social Security revenue. This surplus
revenue was supposed to be saved and invested in marketable
U.S. Treasury bonds that would be held in the trust fund until
the baby boomers began to retire in about 2010. But not one
dime of that money went to Social Security.

The 1983 legislation was sold to the public, and to the
Congress, as a long-term fix for Social Security. The payroll
tax hike was designed to generate large Social Security
surpluses for 30 years, which would be set aside to cover the
increased cost of paying benefits when the boomers retired.

Let's have a look at the events leading up to this
proposal. Reagan and the government had big financial
problems. Supply-side economics was not working like
Reagan had promised. Instead of the lower tax rates
generating more total revenue as the supply-siders claimed
would happen, the revenue generated by the new tax rates was
much lower than the administration had projected. Something
had to be done, so Reagan set for himself a new mission. He
would have to figure out a way to get the additional revenue
he needed from another source.

The mechanism, which allowed the government to
transfer $2.7 trillion from the Social Security fund to the
general fund, over a 30-year period, was the brainchild of
President Ronald Reagan and his advisers, especially Alan
Greenspan. Greenspan played a key role in convincing
Congress and the public to support a hike in the payroll tax

A few years later, Reagan appointed Greenspan to become Chairman of the Federal Reserve System. Since Greenspan's new job was one of the most coveted positions in Washington, many observers have suggested that Greenspan's appointment as Chairman of the Fed may have represented, at least in part, payback for the role he had played in making vast sums of new revenue available to the government.

President Reagan and his advisors knew from the very beginning that the government would soon face a severe cash shortage because of the big cuts in income tax rates. Budget Director, David Stockman had deliberately rigged the computer at the Office of Management and Budget to generate bogus revenue forecasts in an effort to convince Congress to enact Reagan's unaffordable proposed tax cuts. When Stockman first fed the data from Reagan's economic proposals into the computer, he was shocked. The computer forecast that, if Reagan's proposals were enacted into law, massive budget deficits would loom ahead for as far as the eye could see.

Reagan needed a new source of revenue to replace the revenue lost as a result of his unaffordable income tax cuts. He wasn't about to rescind any of the income-tax cuts, but he had another idea. What about raising the payroll tax, and then channeling the new revenue to the general fund, from where it could be spent for other purposes? An increase in Social Security taxes would be easier to enact than a hike in income tax rates, and it would leave Reagan's income-tax cuts undisturbed. Reagan's first step in implementing his strategy was to write to Congressional leaders. His first letter, dated May 21, 1981 included the following:

> As you know, the Social Security System is teetering on the edge of bankruptcy...in the decades ahead its unfunded obligations could run well into the trillions. Unless

we in government are willing to act, a sword of Damocles will soon hang over the welfare of millions of our citizens.

Reagan wrote a follow-up letter to Congressional leaders dated July 18, 1981, which included:

The highest priority of my Administration is restoring the integrity of the Social Security System. Those 35 million Americans who depend on Social Security expect and are entitled to prompt bipartisan action to resolve the current financial problem.

Social Security was definitely not "teetering on the edge of bankruptcy" in 1981, as Reagan claimed in his letter to Congressional leaders. The 1982 National Commission on Social Security Reform, headed by Alan Greenspan, issued its "findings and recommendations" in January 1983. The Commission accurately foresaw major problems for Social Security when the baby boomers began to retire in about 2010. But that was nearly three decades down the road. In addition to the long-term problem of the baby boomers, the Commission found a possible short-term problem for the years 1983-89. But the outlook improved and became favorable for the 1990s and early 2000s. The possible minor problem for the years 1983-1989 was based on very pessimistic economic assumptions. So, at the time Reagan informed Congressional leaders that Social Security was teetering on the edge of bankruptcy, the overall condition of Social Security funding was fairly sound for the next three decades.

Furthermore, Social Security was certainly not Reagan's "highest priority." Reagan had never been a friend of Social Security. He was a hardliner when it came to all government social programs. He called unemployment insurance "a prepaid vacation plan for freeloaders." He said the progressive income tax was "a brainchild of Karl Marx." And, he called welfare recipients "a faceless mass waiting for handouts." Reagan referred to Social Security as a "welfare program" and, during the 1976 Republican Presidential Primary, Reagan proposed making Social Security voluntary, which would have essentially destroyed the program. There is no way that anyone who knew Reagan's record would accept his claim that Social Security was his highest priority. He had always wanted the program eliminated, or at least privatized.

Reagan's scare tactics worked. Congress passed the Social Security Amendments of 1983, which included a hefty increase in the payroll tax rate. The public was led to believe that the surplus money would be saved and invested in marketable U.S. Treasury Bonds, which could later be resold to raise cash with which to pay benefits to the boomers. But that didn't happen. The money was all deposited directly into the general fund and used for non-Social Security purposes. Reagan spent every dime of the surplus Social Security revenue, which came in during his presidency, on general government operations. His successor, George H.W. Bush used the surplus money as a giant slush fund, and both Bill Clinton and George W. Bush looted and spent all of the Social Security surplus revenue that flowed in during their presidencies. So we can't blame the whole problem on Reagan. Reagan was just the one who figured out a way to use Social Security money as general revenue, and his successors just followed his example.

The $2.7 trillion, which is alleged to be in the trust fund, was all spent for wars, tax cuts for the rich, and other government programs. If the money is repaid at some point in the future, we could say it was just "borrowed." But no arrangements have been made to repay the money, and nobody in government is suggesting that the money should be repaid. So, if it is never repaid, the money will definitely have been stolen.

This would not be as serious a problem if Social Security was still running annual surpluses. But Social Security ran its last annual surplus in 2009, and began running permanent annual deficits in 2010. The cost of paying full Social Security benefits for 2010 exceeded Social Security's total tax revenue by $49 billion. So how did the government pay full Social Security benefits in 2010? They borrowed $49 billion from China, or one of our other creditors. And the amount that will have to be borrowed in future years will become larger and larger. If the trust fund had not been looted, there would be $2.7 trillion of marketable U.S. Treasury bonds in the fund that could be sold in the open market for cash. But the trust fund doesn't hold a dime's worth of marketable real assets of any kind.

That's why President Obama warned during the debt-ceiling crisis of 2011 that Social Security checks could not go out on time unless the dispute was settled, because "there might not be enough money in the coffers." The grandiose lie that the Social Security Administration, the AARP, and the NCPSSM, repeatedly tells the public is outrageous. They continue to say that Social Security has enough money to pay full benefits for another 20 years, without any government action, when Social Security cannot pay full benefits for a single year without borrowing money. The IOUs in the trust fund are not marketable, and they have no monetary value. They are essentially worthless!

Between 1981 and 1986, the United States was transformed from the world's largest lender to the world's largest borrower. Although most Americans were never made aware of this historic role reversal for the United States, we can be sure that our adversaries around the world took note of it. At the very same time that President Ronald Reagan was building up our military strength to enhance our security and status in the world, our economic strength was waning as we saw our role as the world's largest lender being replaced with the dubious distinction of being the world's largest borrower.

One might have expected our leaders to be so concerned about America's new status as the world's largest borrower, that they would have put a high priority on taking actions that would help undo the role reversal. But they did not. They seemed to be comfortable with their "borrow and spend" approach to handling the government's finances.

The 1984 presidential election campaign showed just how naïve, and economically illiterate the American electorate is. It also demonstrated how a charismatic leader, like Ronald Reagan, can convince the masses to ignore facts, and the advice of experts, and persuade them to follow him wherever he leads, even if it is over the edge of a cliff.

During the 1980 campaign, Reagan had promised that his large tax cuts would lead to a balanced budget by 1984. Instead, the 1984 budget had a deficit of $185.3 billion. Furthermore, the national debt, which had taken 200 years to reach the $1 trillion mark, had increased to $1.56 trillion by 1984, and it was racing toward the $2 trillion mark.

The budget was so out of control that almost every mainstream economist in the country would probably have argued that the 1981 tax cuts were too big and had to be adjusted. Economic advisers to former Vice President Walter Mondale, who was the Democratic presidential nominee in 1984, convinced Mondale that a tax increase was absolutely necessary to bring the runaway deficits under control.

Mondale apparently thought he could be honest with the American people about the deficit problem and the need for a special deficit-reduction tax. So Mondale told the voters that a tax increase was inevitable, no matter whether he or Reagan was elected. Mondale said:

> Mr. Reagan will raise your taxes and so will I. He won't tell you, I just did."

Although Mondale pledged that every dollar of the revenue from the proposed new tax would be used to reduce the deficit, and not a single dollar of it would be used for new spending, his honesty turned out to be a disastrous strategy. Reagan ridiculed Mondale's tax proposal and promised that he would bring prosperity and balanced budgets without raising taxes.

One might think that, since Reagan had not kept his 1980 promises, and since the runaway deficits were alarming economists and many others, the voters might have been hesitant to vote for Reagan again. But they were not. On election day, Reagan won 49 states, and Mondale won his home state of Minnesota by only 3,800 votes! It was one of the most lopsided landslide victories in history. Historians may eventually decide that it was also one of the greatest mistakes the American people, as a whole, had ever made.

America was on the wrong track in 1984. After 200 years of following reasonably responsible fiscal policies, that had made America the economic envy of the world, the nation had gone on a four-year fling with deficit financing. Instead of living within our means as a nation, we were following a policy of borrowing from future generations in order to spend more than we could afford. It should have been clear to almost everyone that the United States government could not go on, indefinitely, spending more than its income. But apparently it was not.

The 1984 election offered the opportunity for an informed electorate to change the course of history for the better through the democratic process. If the public had been educated in economics, they would have realized that Reagan's flirtation with supply-side economic theory had been disastrous. The supply-side theory had been tested, and it had flunked the test miserably. But America did not have an informed electorate. The public was economically illiterate.

The surplus Social Security revenue, generated by the 1983 payroll tax hike, started out small, but escalated rapidly. Although only about $84.5 billion of Social Security surplus came in during the Reagan presidency, during the four years of George H.W. Bush's presidency, there was an additional $211.7 billion in Social Security surplus revenue. Every penny of the surplus from both the Reagan and Bush administrations was spent on non-Social Security programs.

The surplus money should have been saved and invested in marketable U.S. Treasury bonds, which could have later been resold in order to raise cash with which to pay benefits. Instead, the surplus Social Security revenue was spent just as if it were general revenue. Bush, who had said during the campaign, *"Read my lips. No new taxes,"* did not need to raise taxes when he could spend money from the Social Security surplus at will.

A few courageous United States Senators tried to nip the Social Security fraud in the bud early on by speaking out against it. The three most vocal senators on the issue were Senator Daniel Patrick Moynihan (D-NY) Senator Ernest (Fritz) Hollings (D-SC), and Senator Harry Reid(D-NV). On October 13, 1989, Senator Hollings lambasted the Bush administration for its use of Social Security surplus dollars for funding other programs. Excerpts from that speech are reproduced below from the Congressional Record {Page: S13411}.

...The most reprehensible fraud in this great jambalaya
of frauds is the systematic and total ransacking of the Social

Security trust fund in order to mask the true size of the deficit. The public fully supported enactment of hefty new Social Security taxes in 1983 to ensure the retirement program's long-term solvency and credibility. The promise was that today's huge surpluses would be set safely aside in a trust fund to provide for the baby-boomer retirees in the next century.

Well, look again. The Treasury is siphoning off every dollar of the Social Security surplus to meet current operating expenses of the Government. The hard fact is that, in the next century, the Social Security system will find itself paying out vastly more in benefits than it is taking in through payroll taxes. And the American people will wake up to the reality that those IOU's in the trust fund vault are a 21st century version of Confederate banknotes."

Nearly a year later, the looting of the trust fund was continuing unchanged. On October 9, 1990, Senator Harry Reid expressed his outrage at the practice during a senate speech. Excerpts from the speech are reproduced below from the Congressional Record {Page: S14759}.

"The discussion is are we as a country violating a trust by spending Social Security trust fund moneys for some purpose other than for which they were intended. The obvious answer is yes...

The trust funds resources are there for the well-being of those who have paid into the Social Security System. We should use those resources to see that Social Security recipients are treated well but also treated fairly and treated equitably.

It is time for Congress, I think, to take its hands—and I add the President in on that—off the Social Security surpluses. Stop hiding the horrible truth of the fiscal irresponsibility that we have talked about here the past 2 weeks. It is time to return those dollars to the hands of those who earned them—the Social Security beneficiaries and future beneficiaries...

I think that is a very good illustration of what I was talking about, embezzlement, thievery. Because that, Mr. President, is what we are talking about here...On that chart in emblazoned red letters is what has been taking place here, embezzlement. During the period of growth we have had during the past 10 years, the growth has been from two sources: One, a large credit card with no limits on it, and, two, we have been stealing money from the Social Security recipients of this country.

Out of this heated debate on the issue of government misappropriation of Social Security money, came Senator Daniel Patrick Moynihan's proposal to cut Social Security taxes in order to deny the government access to the tempting surplus Social Security money. Senator Moynihan, who had been a strong supporter of the 1983 efforts to strengthen the Social Security system, was outraged that, instead of being used to build up the size of the Social Security Trust Fund for future retirees, as was intended, the Social Security surplus was being used to pay for general government spending.

Because Moynihan believed the American people were being deceived and betrayed, he proposed undoing the 1983 legislation by cutting Social Security taxes and returning the system to a "pay-as-you-go" basis which would have provided only enough revenue to take care of current retirees. Moynihan's position was that, if the government could not keep its hands out of the Social Security cookie jar, the jar should be emptied so there would be no Social Security surplus

President George H. W. Bush was furious over Moynihan's proposal. In response to reporters' questions, Bush replied, "It is an effort to get me to raise taxes on the American people by the charade of cutting them, or cut benefits, and I am not going to do it to the older people of this country."

But President Bush was in fact taking money from a fund that was supposed to be used to provide for "the older people of this country" and using it to fund general government. Despite the strong efforts, way back in 1990, to put an end to the raiding of the Social Security trust fund, President George H.W. Bush continued to loot and spend every dollar of the Social Security surplus.

Even though Social Security funds are required, by federal law, to be kept separate from other funds, Presidents Reagan and George H.W. Bush treated them just like general revenue, and spent every dollar on other government programs. I would like to be able to think that our two-party system would have eliminated the practice whenever the next Democratic president entered the White House. But it did not. President Clinton seemed to think that, if his two predecessors had gotten by with violating the law and treating the Social Security surpluses as general revenue, then he could probably get by with it too. And he did.

During the 2000 presidential election campaign, both Al Gore and George W. Bush publicly acknowledged the past looting of Social Security money, and they both pledged to end the practice. But George W. Bush blatantly ignored both his pledge and federal law and continued the looting just like his three predecessors.

Sadly, there is not a single dollar of real money or any other kind of real asset in the trust fund. It contains only government IOUs that serve as accounting records of how much money the government has taken from Social Security and spent for other purposes.

The American people hear over and over from government officials that the Social Security money was invested in government bonds. That is a big lie. The money was not invested in anything, because it was spent as general revenue at the time it came in. Money can be saved and invested, or it can be spent. However, money cannot be both spent and invested. Once the money is spent, there is nothing left to invest.

The way the government has been able to deceive the public on this issue is through accounting gimmickry. The government created a special type of certificate available only to the trust funds. The certificates are called "special issue Treasuries" or "special issue Treasury bonds." But they are not real bonds in the sense that most people use the term. They are simply accounting devices for keeping track of how much money the government owes to Social Security. They are nothing more than IOUs.

In a Washington speech on January 21, 2005, David Walker, Comptroller General of the GAO, sought to make it clear, once and for all, that the Social Security trust fund contains no real assets. He said,

> There are no stocks or bonds or real estate in the trust fund. It has nothing of real value to draw down.

If the trust fund held regular public issue Treasury bonds like everyone else invests in, there would be no problem. The bonds could be sold in the open market at any time for full market value. The trust fund is allowed to hold marketable bonds and has held some public issue marketable Treasury bonds in the past. However, it does not now hold any such bonds.

The special issue certificates are not marketable and thus cannot be bought or sold for even a penny on the dollar. They are totally worthless accounting devices. During President George W. Bush's campaign to partially privatize Social Security, he became desperate to find new ammunition with which to convince the public that Social Security faces real problems. Finally, he decided to tell the truth about the trust fund.

During a speech in Pennsylvania on February 10, 2005, President Bush made a very candid statement about government Social Security practices. He said,

> Every dime that goes in from payroll taxes is spent. It's spent on retirees, and if there's excess, it's spent on government programs. The only thing that Social Security .

has is a pile of IOUs from one part of government to the next.

During a speech in West Virginia on April 5, 2005, . President Bush said,

> There is no trust fund, just IOUs that I saw firsthand that future generations will pay—will pay for either in higher taxes, or reduced benefits, or cuts to other critical government programs.

Despite these definitive statements by the President and the Comptroller General, we continued to be told that all Social Security surplus money was safe and sound, because it was invested in "government bonds."

None of the Social Security surplus money is invested in anything. It was all spent at the time it came in, so there was nothing left to invest.

CHAPTER FIVE

ECONOMIC POLICIES DURING THE REAGAN-BUSH YEARS

During the 1980 presidential election campaign, Ronald Reagan made one of the most irresistible promises that has ever been made in any presidential election campaign.

Reagan opened his speech as follows:

"If I am elected President, I will cut your tax rates by 10 percent during my first year in office."

The crowd was allowed to cheer for only a moment before Reagan raised his hand and said,

"Wait a minute! I'm not done. If elected President, I will cut your tax rates another 10 percent during my second year in office."

This time Reagan allowed the crowd to applaud a little longer before raising his hand again to quiet them. He then said,

"I'm still not done. I have an encore. During my third year in office, I will cut your taxes an additional 10 percent. I will cut tax rates by 30 percent during my first three years, and we will have a balanced budget by 1984!"

This time the gifted orator allowed the crowd to scream and applaud as long as they wished.

Reagan made this same promise over and over as he traveled around the country in 1980. He would be Santa Claus, the tooth fairy, and all other good things, wrapped in a single package. How could American voters resist such a promise?

Reagan began his tax-cut promises during the Republican primary campaign in which George H.W. Bush was also a candidate for the Republican nomination for president. How did Bush react to Reagan's promise of a 30 percent cut in tax rates over three years? He ridiculed it.

He referred to Reagan's tax proposal as "voodoo economic policy," and "economic madness." Reagan won the primary campaign and became the Republican nominee for President who would oppose President Jimmy Carter in the fall 1980 campaign.

Reagan continued to promise to cut tax rates by 30 percent over a three-year period throughout the fall campaign. Jimmy Carter argued that such a policy would plunge the federal budget into deficits and also fuel inflation. Mainstream economists warned against the reckless Reagan plan. Even some fiscally conservative Republican members of Congress voiced opposition to the plan.

What was my reaction to Reagan's proposal? Shock, disbelief, and fear for the nation's future, if Reagan got elected and followed through with his crazy promise. Never before during my lifetime had I seen such an outrageous and dangerous proposal come from the mouth of someone who might become president. I don't believe that Ronald Reagan would have been able to defeat Carter without the big tax-cut promise. Carter had the Iranian hostage crisis working against him, but, even with that, I don't think Reagan could have won the election without the big "gift" he was promising the American people. You can buy almost anything if you've got enough money. And Reagan was promising to take a big chunk of the federal government's tax revenue and give it back to the people, if they elected him.

As election day neared, I became increasingly convinced that the big tax-cut promise was just too much of an incentive for many voters to ignore. I thought Reagan would probably be elected, but I hoped that he would renege on his promise. Surely he would listen to mainstream economists and spare the economy the damage that the massive tax cuts would inflict, if enacted into law.

On election night, once it became clear that Reagan had won, I received a phone call from one of my university colleagues who shared my concerns about what a Reagan presidency might mean. When I picked up the phone, Vic's first words were, "Well, Allen, he fooled a lot of people. But he didn't fool you and me, did he?"

Reagan's tax cut proposal was part of a new economic theory called supply-side economics. This new theory received most of its support from politicians and other non-economists. Usually, new economic theories require years of debate and testing before they stand a chance of being implemented as a part of government economic policy, even when they are the product of some of the greatest minds in the field. But, because the ideas of the supply-side supporters were so compatible with the political philosophy of Ronald Reagan, the new, untested theory was to become the cornerstone of Reagan's economic policy.

Most professional economists had never heard the term "supply-side economics" until Ronald Reagan. announced his support for it in the 1980 primary campaign. I had a Ph.D. degree in economics and had been teaching the subject to college students for more than a dozen years at the time Reagan introduced the concept to the world. Yet, I had never seen any reference to the concept in any of the professional literature, and it was not included in any textbook that I had ever seen.

There is good reason for this. The theory almost came out of nowhere. Robert Merry and Kenneth Bacon stated in a February 18, 1981 *Wall Street Journal* article, "Capturing the Executive Branch of government was an amazing victory for the supply-side movement, which hardly existed a mere eight years ago." And so it was. Never before had an economic theory so new, so untested, and with so little support from professional economists as a whole, been accepted and pushed by the federal government.

According to Merry and Bacon, supply-side economics became a political movement when the ideas of Arthur Laffer, of the University of Southern California, and Robert Mundell, of Columbia, captured the imagination of Jude Wanniski, an editorial writer for the *Wall Street Journal,* who reportedly sought receptive Washington politicians and finally found one in Representative Jack Kemp of New York. In 1977, Representative Kemp, along with Senator William Roth of Delaware, coauthored the Kemp-Roth Bill to slash individual income tax rates by 30 percent over a three-year period. Mr. Kemp then reportedly set out to convert Mr. Reagan, whom he considered the most receptive of the potential presidents.

The ideas and objectives of the supply-siders were very compatible with Mr. Reagan's own political philosophy, so it was not difficult to convert him to the new economic theories. Thus, Reagan's pledge to support passage of the Kemp-Roth Bill and call for a 30 percent cut in tax rates over a three-year period became the most popular promise of his campaign and undoubtedly played a major role in his big win.

Supply-side economists emphasized the interrelationship between the total supply of goods and services and the government's taxing and spending policies. They believed that tax rates had become so high that there was a disincentive to work or produce. Some also argued that subsidies to the poor were so generous that they discouraged the poor from increasing their earnings for fear their government aid would be reduced.

President Reagan's proposed 30 percent cut in tax rates, over a three-year period, was based on the argument that such a tax cut would result in a substantial increase in the total supply of goods and services produced. The argument was based on the belief that tax rates were so high that many individuals took more lengthy vacations, accepted less overtime work, and retired earlier than they would if tax rates were substantially lower. In addition, the supply-siders argued that the high tax rates discouraged business people from pursuing promising but risky investment opportunities because, even if they were successful, the government would take much of the profits in higher taxes.

These beliefs led supply-siders to argue that a massive tax cut, such as Reagan's proposal for a 30 percent cut in tax rates, over a three-year period, would lead to more revenue, not less. Here is where the theories left the real world and entered fantasyland. The American people were being told that they could have their cake and eat it too, and they loved it. According to Reagan, he could cut tax rates by 30 percent and collect more revenue than before the tax cut. In fact, President Reagan promised that if Congress would just enact his proposal the federal budget would be balanced by 1984, and he would simultaneously reduce both unemployment and inflation.

Congress did enact the President's economic program, including the tax-cut proposal, which had been reduced (at the request of Budget Director David Stockman) from a 30 percent cut to a 25 percent cut in personal income tax rates, over a three-year period. However, the country soon learned that the promised simultaneous reduction in inflation and unemployment rates was not to be. Inflation did come down, as the economy plunged into the worst recession in half a century. The civilian unemployment rate climbed to 10.7 percent in December 1982, the highest since the Great Depression of the 1930s. Millions of Americans lost their jobs, and the annual civilian unemployment rate remained above 9.5 percent for both 1982 and 1983.

As the economy recovered from the severe recession, President Reagan argued that his economic policies were working and the economy was headed toward true and lasting prosperity. On the surface things did look encouraging. The unemployment rate was gradually declining, and inflation was remaining low. However, a huge cloud hung over the optimism because of the unprecedented size of the federal budget deficits, and the rapid growth in the national debt.

A president, who had promised that his policies would lead to a balanced budget by 1984, instead gave us record budget deficits and a doubling of the national debt in six years. The Reagan administration added more to the national debt in six years than all the other presidents, from George Washington through Jimmy Carter combined, had added in nearly 200 years. The federal budget deficits soared from $73.8 billion in fiscal 1980 to a record $221.2 billion in fiscal 1986.

Nations, like individuals, cannot indefinitely live beyond their means. While much of the borrowed money came from Americans who invested in government securities, substantial amounts of foreign capital was used to finance the huge budget deficits.

Why were the basic economic problems allowed to grow to such disastrous proportions? The primary reason was that, for the first time in modern history, an American president chose to almost totally ignore the advice of professional economists, both inside and outside of the administration. Unless an economist could be found whose advice was compatible with Reaganomics, the administration simply ignored the advice. It would have been bad enough if the President had just ignored the advice of outside economists and had listened to his own handpicked economists. However, he ignored both groups.

President Reagan was required to select competent economic advisers to meet the legal requirement of the Employment Act of 1946. One of the provisions of this act required the President to appoint a Council of Economic

Advisers so that he would always have close access to the advice of some of the best professional economists in the country. Thus, President Reagan did appoint three economists to his Council of Economic Advisers. Unfortunately, however, he chose not to listen to their advice and allowed people with little or no professional training in economics to formulate his economic policies.

When Murray Weidenbaum, Reagan's first Chairman of the Council of Economic Advisers, re-signed early in the administration, the President had the opportunity to search the nation for his type of economist as Weidenbaum's replacement. Finally, in 1982, he selected Martin Feldstein, a Harvard economist, as his new Chairman.

Mr. Feldstein took his appointment seriously, and he expected to influence economic policy within the administration. He immediately began to warn the President about the gigantic federal budget deficits and insisted that something be done to reduce them. However, Feldstein soon learned that he had been appointed only to fill the position, and that his advice was not going to be taken seriously.

When Feldstein warned of the deficit dangers in the annual Economic Report of the President, Treasury Secretary, Donald Regan, a non-economist who was playing a major role in economic policy making, told Congress, "As far as I'm concerned, you can throw it (The Economic Report) away." Feldstein had warned that the deficits, if not curtailed soon, could devastate the nation's economy. Feldstein had argued that taxes should be raised as a way of reducing the projected $180 billion fiscal 1985 deficit. (As it turned out the actual on-budget deficit for fiscal 1985 was $212.7 billion.)

Earlier, in 1983, Feldstein had said, "If Congress doesn't act soon to cut future deficits, interest rates will remain high and weaken the economy. Future back-to-back $200 billion deficits will increase the national debt . by an additional $1 trillion over the next few years, eventually forcing the government to implement drastic spending cuts and tax increases."

When Feldstein, out of frustration, began giving public speeches on the subject of the dangerous deficits, he was ordered to submit his speeches to the White House for prior approval before giving them. The final straw fell when, just a short time before Feldstein was scheduled to appear on an ABC news show on Sunday February 5, 1984, he was ordered by the White House to cancel the scheduled appearance because his comments might embarrass the administration.

When Feldstein left the administration in 1984, President Reagan proposed abolishing the Council of Economic Advisers because he felt it served no useful purpose. When Congress created the Council of Economic Advisers with the Employment Act of 1946, the main concern was that all future presidents have close access to the best professionally trained economists available, in order to avoid major economic policy mistakes. President Reagan, who had demonstrated repeatedly, throughout his presidency, through his speeches and actions, that he had almost no understanding of how the American economy operated, wanted no part of any such arrangement. He would rely on non-economists who shared his political philosophy to formulate the economic policy of the nation.

The chief architects of Reagan economic policy, in the early years of the administration, were Treasury Secretary Donald Regan and Budget director David Stockman. Mr. Regan, who was the former head of the Merrill Lynch stock brokerage firm, had business experience, but he was not an economist. Many people who are quite successful at business have very little understanding of how the national economy operates. Budget Director Stockman, who was probably the chief architect of economic policy in the early days, had absolutely no formal training in economics. Yet, despite the warnings of many outside prominent economists—including recipients of the Nobel Prize in economics—as well as his own hand-picked Harvard economist, Martin Feldstein, President Reagan allowed non-economists to formulate national economic policy.

Similar actions in other sectors of our economy would be a crime. Suppose a person who had never attended medical school performed surgery on a patient. What would happen to such a person? He would probably be sentenced to serve time in prison because of the threat he posed to this single individual. Yet, people without training in economics were allowed to perform radical surgery on a national economy that affected the lives of nearly 240 million Americans. The damage done to the economy by these people will be felt for a long time to come.

In order to understand why a president would ignore the advice of most professional economists and allow non-economists to formulate economic policy, one must understand that the goals of the Reagan Revolution were more political than economic in nature. President Reagan came to Washington, determined to reverse the political direction that this nation had been following for 40 years. The new President had hated the growth in government social programs that had evolved over the previous 40 years, and he was determined to move the nation in a new direction.

Reagan wanted to reduce the size of the federal government and the role it played in the American economy. He was determined to reduce spending on social programs and increase spending on national defense. And he was determined to reduce taxes, especially for the very wealthy. When supply-side advocates approached him with the Kemp-Roth tax cut proposal and promised that it would lead to a stronger economy, as well as accomplish his political objectives, the President couldn't have been happier.

From that time on, mainstream economists and mainstream economic policies would play little role in the Reagan administration. If the economic advice was not compatible with the goals of the Reagan Revolution, it was to be ignored.

The promise of large cuts in tax rates would almost certainly increase Reagan's chances of making it to the White House, as well as put him in a good strategic position for downsizing the government, which was a primary goal of Reaganomics. He thought that, if there were less revenue available, there would have to be sharp reductions in spending.

But Reagan had underestimated how easy it would be to just borrow funds to replace the revenue lost from the tax cut. In his first televised address to the nation, on February 5, 1981, Reagan declared:

> There were always those who told us that taxes couldn't be cut until spending was reduced. Well, you know we can lecture our children about extravagance until we run out of voice and breath. Or we can cut their extravagance by simply reducing their allowance.

In early January of 1981, Budget Director, David Stockman, who was 34 years old and lacked any formal training in economics, began to formulate plans for the first Reagan budget. When Stockman and his staff fed the data of the proposed Reagan economic program into a computer that was programmed as a model of the nation's economic behavior, and instructed the computer to estimate the impact of Reagan's program on the federal budget, he was shocked. The computer predicted that if the President went ahead with his promised three-year tax reduction and his increase in defense spending, the Reagan Administration would be faced with a series of federal budget deficits without precedent. The projections ranged from an $82 billion deficit in 1982 to $116 billion in 1984—the year the President had promised to balance the budget. Stockman knew that if those were the numbers included in President Reagan's first budget message the following month, the financial markets would be panicked, and Congress would be unlikely to approve the budget.

The young Stockman, untrained in economics, decided that the assumptions programmed into the computer by earlier economists were not correct. So he and his team discarded orthodox premises of how the economy would behave and reprogrammed the computer with new assumptions that would give them the projected balanced budget that the President had promised for 1984. However, later, when the nonpartisan Congressional Budget Office projected continuing large budget deficits instead of a balanced budget by 1984, there seemed to be a problem of credibility with either Stockman's numbers or those of the Congressional Budget Office. When President Reagan was asked by reporters why the two sets of projections were so different, he charged that the Congressional Budget Office and members of Congress endorsing the CBO projections were trying to shoot down his economic program by using "phony" figures.

Phony figures were indeed being used, but not by the Congressional Budget Office. Of course, the Congress and the public had no way of knowing at the time that Stockman had rigged the computer at the Office of Management and Budget (OMB) in order to show a projected balanced budget for 1984. It was not until the publication of the infamous article, "The Education of David Stockman." by William Greider in the December 1981 issue of *The Atlantic Monthly* that the public learned the whole story.

Much was learned about the early days of the

Reagan Administration from that article, which almost cost Stockman his job. When Stockman's appointment as budget director first seemed likely, he had agreed to meet with William Greider, an assistant managing editor at the *Washington Post*, from time to time and relate, off the record, his private account of the great political struggle ahead. The particulars of these conversations were not to be reported until later, after the President's program had been approved by Congress. Stockman and Greider met for regular conversations over breakfast for eight months, and these conversations provided the basis for Greider's article in *The Atlantic Monthly*.

The article became a political bombshell when it was published. In addition to the revelation of the computer rigging in order to get budget projections that could be sold to the Congress, Stockman asserted that the supply-side theory was not a new economic theory at all, but just new language and argument for the doctrine of the old Republican orthodoxy known as "trickle down" economics. Basically, this doctrine holds that the government should give tax cuts to the top brackets; the wealthiest individuals and the largest enterprises, and let the good effects "trickle down" through the economy to reach everyone else. According to Stockman, when one stripped away the new rhetoric, emphasizing across-the-board cuts, the supply-side theory was really new clothes for the unpopular doctrine of the old Republican orthodoxy. Stockman said, "It's kind of hard to sell 'trickle down,' so the supply-side formula was the only way to get a tax policy that was really 'trickle down.' Supply-side is 'trickle down' theory."

Stockman said that the Kemp-Roth tax cut bill was a Trojan horse to bring down the top rate. "The hard part of the supply-side tax cut is dropping the top rate from 73 to 50 percent—the rest of it is a secondary matter," Stockman said. "The original argument was that the top bracket was too high, and that's having the most devastating effect on the economy. Then, the general argument was that, in order to make this palatable as a political matter, you had to bring down all brackets. But, I mean, Kemp-Roth was always a Trojan horse to bring down the top rate."

Many people were misled by the 25 percent cut in personal income tax rates that was enacted during the first year of the Reagan Presidency. Many thought it meant a 25 percent cut in the amount of taxes each individual paid. But this wasn't true. People who were in the 70 percent bracket, which was cut to 50 percent, saved $20 on each $100 of taxable income. However, a person who was in the 16 percent bracket would have his or her tax rate cut from 16 percent to 12 percent and would save only $4 on each $100 of taxable income. In other words, the tax cut benefited the rich to a much greater extent than the poor. In fact, because of the substantial cuts in programs that benefited primarily the poor, most poor people were actually hurt by the tax cut.

Studies have shown that persons with an income of $10,000 just about broke even. In other words, any benefits from the tax cuts were offset by losses resulting from cutbacks in government programs that benefited them. People with incomes below $10,000 were worse off after the tax cut, and people with incomes above $10,000 benefited from the tax cut. The higher one's income, the greater the benefit from the tax cut. For example, a person with a taxable income of $500,000 would pay $100,000 less in taxes as a result of the tax cut.

Aside from the effects of the tax cut on the economy, many social scientists believe that the benefits gained by the rich caused undue hardships on the poor. For example, in an effort to save money on the social security program without cutting benefits to the masses, the administration launched a review of recipients receiving social security disability benefits and decided in many cases that the people were not severely enough disabled to warrant continued disability benefits. Thus, at a time when the economy was plunging into a severe recession and many able-bodied workers were unable to find jobs, many people who had become dependent upon Social Security disability payments as their only means of support suddenly had their benefits cut off. The issue was brought to the public's attention when a man in Pennsylvania went down to the local Social Security office with a shotgun and committed suicide in front of Social Security workers. When police went to the man's house they found a note on the kitchen table that read, "They're playing God. They've taken away my Social Security benefits." Eventually, Congress intervened and brought a halt to the cut off of disability benefits.

Many programs designed to help the poor were cut or eliminated in an effort to afford the big tax cut, much of which went to the very rich. Whether this is right or wrong involves value judgments. However, many Americans who like to think of this country as a fair and compassionate nation feel there was little evidence of concern for the problems of the poor in the Reagan economic program.

As President Reagan ended his term of office he claimed that his administration had been one of prosperity. However, the record shows otherwise. President Reagan had the worst unemployment record of any modern president. During his first four-year term, the average annual unemployment rate was 8.6 percent—7.6 percent in 1981, 9.7 percent in 1982, 9.6 percent in 1983, and 7.5 percent in 1984. At no other time since the Great Depression of the 1930s had the unemployment rate ever been as high as 8.6 percent even for a single year, let alone for a 4-year average. If we look at Mr. Reagan's full 8-year Presidency, the average annual unemployment rate is 7.5 percent. Since the Great Depression, only in 1975 and

1976, during the Ford Presidency, has the unemployment rate been as high, in even a single year, as Reagan's 8-year average unemployment rate.

President Reagan tried to blame the high unemployment of the early years of his term on former President Jimmy Carter. He claimed the economy was already in a recession when he took office. This is not true. President Carter added 10 million jobs to the economy during his four years in office. The unemployment rate was 7.7 percent during the last year of the Ford Administration. During the Carter Presidency, the unemployment rate was reduced to 5.8 percent in 1979, before the economy entered a mild recession in January of 1980, which began driving unemployment back up. However, United States Commerce Department statistics clearly show that the Carter recession hit bottom two months later in March 1980, and the economy began to expand again. The economy was expanding and unemployment was falling when President Reagan took office. However, the economy was very fragile, having just come out of a recession, and it was extremely important that the proper economic policies be followed to prevent the economy from slipping into a new recession.

The policies of the Reagan administration played a major role in the severe recession. The President called upon the Federal Reserve System to pursue a tight-money policy, he cut domestic spending, and he failed to implement his promised first-year 10 percent cut in tax rates that was to have been retroactive to January 1, 1981. The fragile economy could not withstand such policies. Budget Director, David Stockman, who had begun to worry about forthcoming deficits, convinced the President to reduce his first-year tax cut from 10 percent to 5 percent and delay its implementation until October 1.

Thus, instead of the 10 percent cut in tax rates for the entire year that had been planned, there was a cut of only 5 percent, and it was in effect for only the last 3 months of the year. This translates into a 1.25 percent average tax cut for the entire year instead of the planned 10 percent cut. This, combined with the tight money policy and the cuts in domestic spending, was more than the economy could stand. It plunged the economy into the worst recession since the Great Depression of the 1930s, causing millions of Americans to lose their jobs.

The severe recession of 1981-82 did not have to happen. It was caused by government policies. If the President had implemented the planned 10 percent tax cut in January and called on the Fed to pursue an easier-money policy, it is my belief that there would not have been a recession and all the suffering that accompanied it. Of course, the economy could not have withstood the planned two additional 10 percent cuts in the two succeeding years without problems of deficits and inflation. But the first year's planned 10 percent tax cut was very much needed at the time to stimulate the economy.

President Reagan claimed that he brought inflation under control. However, Reagan could not take credit for reducing inflation unless he was willing to accept the blame for the recession. The inflation rate came down for two reasons. First and foremost, there is no surer way to reduce inflation than to throw the economy into a severe recession. With aggregate demand falling, it is difficult for prices to rise. As more and more people become unemployed, and lose their spending power, sellers are forced to reduce their prices, or at least stop raising them, in order to make sales.

Secondly, much of the inflation of the 1970s was caused by soaring energy prices. The price of crude oil rose from $3 a barrel to $33 a barrel during the period 1973 to 1980. This caused an increase in the price of almost everything because energy makes up a part of the production cost and much of the transportation cost of most products. Just as President Reagan took office, a glut in world oil supplies developed, making it impossible for crude oil prices to rise further.

Even if prices had remained at a steady level of $33 per barrel, there would have been no further upward pressures on prices resulting from the energy crisis. But prices of crude oil actually dropped substantially during the Reagan administration, helping to offset price increases of other items and keep the inflation rate low.

The national debt doubled from $1 trillion to $2 trillion during the first six years of the Reagan Presidency, and was more than $2.6 trillion when Reagan left office. However, things were to get much worse during the next four years under President Bush.

Some observers had high hopes that Bush would abandon the economic policies of Reagan that had submerged the government so deep into red ink. After all, Bush had referred to Reagan's proposed economic package as "voodoo economics" during the 1980 primary campaign. It was understandable that Bush would have to support Reagan's polices while he was Reagan's vice president, but once he was elected to his own term as president, Bush was free to take a different course.

But Bush did not change course. He continued to follow the politically popular, but economically disastrous, policies that had already done so much damage to the financial condition of the government. During Bush's four years as president, the on-budget deficit (excluding Social Security) averaged more than $286 billion per year! And when Bush left office, the national debt which had been only $1 trillion dollars at the beginning of the Reagan-Bush administration had soared above the $4 trillion mark.

One accomplishment during the Reagan-Bush years that is very dear to the hearts of conservatives was the reduction in revenue that necessitated smaller government. Although Reaganomics is usually associated with the theories of supply-side economics, a more accurate description of Reaganomics is the policies that were based primarily on the personal economic position, beliefs, and assumptions of Ronald Reagan. When the supply-siders tried to convince Reagan to endorse their plan for a 30 percent cut in income tax rates they had no problem at all. The big tax cut was totally in line with Reagan's number one goal. That goal was to reduce the size of the federal government.

Reagan said over and over that the economic problems of America were the result of too much government. He wanted to trim the size of the federal government as much as possible, and he seemed to believe that if taxes were cut severely, there would be a corresponding cut in federal spending. In Reagan's first inaugural address he said:

> ...great as our tax burden is, it has not kept pace with public spending... for decades, we have piled deficit upon deficit, mortgaging our future and our children's future for the temporary convenience of the present. To continue this long trend is to guarantee tremendous social, cultural, political, and economic upheavals.
>
> You and I, as individuals, can, by borrowing, live beyond our means, but for only a limited period of time. Why, then, should we think that collectively, as a nation, we are not bound by that same limitation?
>
> ...It is my intention to curb the size and influence of the Federal establishment and to demand recognition of the distinction between the powers granted to the Federal Government and those reserved to the States or to the people. It is no coincidence that our present troubles parallel and are proportionate to the intervention and intrusion in our lives that result from unnecessary and excessive growth of government.

With the benefit of hindsight, we can now see just how contradictory Reagan's words and actions were.

When he said, "For decades, we have piled deficit upon deficit, mortgaging our future and our children's future for the temporary convenience of the present," a reasonable person would likely conclude that Reagan was being critical of large government deficits. One would then further conclude that Reagan intended to follow policies that would result in smaller deficits than in the past. Instead, Reagan gave us budget deficits of a magnitude not even imaginable in the past, and he tripled the size of the national debt during his eight years as President.

Prior to Reagan's presidency, we had never had a budget deficit as high as $100 billion, and only two years with deficits in the $70 billion range. In 1976, during the Ford administration, the deficit was $70.5 billion. In 1980, during the Carter administration, the deficit was $72.2 billion. Both of these deficits were primarily the result of economic recessions that reduced the government's tax revenue. The average annual deficit for the entire decade of the 1970s was only $35.38 billion. These are the deficits that Reagan was so critical of—the ones he said had mortgaged our future and our children's future."

The average deficit of $168.87 for the entire decade of the 1980s dwarfed the average deficit for the decade of the 1970s. The annual deficits soared under both President Reagan and President George Herbert Walker Bush. The 1982 deficit of $120.1 billion represented the first time in history that the deficit had topped the $100 billion mark. The very next year, in 1983, the deficit exceeded the $200 billion mark, weighing in at $208 billion.

The longer the Reagan economic policies were in place, the larger the budget deficits became. In 1992, the last year of the George H.W. Bush administration, the budget deficit was an astronomical $340 billion! The national debt, which was less than $1 trillion when Reagan assumed the Presidency, had quadrupled to more than $4 trillion by the time George H. W. Bush turned over the reigns of power to Bill Clinton.

Clinton pushed through his controversial deficit-reduction package without the vote of a single Republican member of Congress, amid outcries that Clinton's plan would devastate both the economy and the budget. The budget deficits gradually and steadily declined throughout the Clinton years, finally resulting in a tiny surplus of $1.8 billion in 1999 and a sizeable surplus of $86.6 billion in 2000.

In summary, before the introduction of Reaganomics, the nation had accumulated approximately $1 trillion in national debt throughout our entire history. Twelve years later, the debt had quadrupled. The economic malpractice of the Reagan-Bush years will have a negative impact for generations to come. We couldn't change that, but we could certainly have insisted that, from that point on, national economic policies should be based on sound economic principles that are supported by the majority of mainstream economists.

Ronald Reagan, the great communicator, had the charisma to get reelected despite the poor performance of the economy and the huge deficits. He was often referred to as the "Teflon" president, because very little seemed to stick to him personally. He had a way of deflecting the responsibility for problems to other people. And, as the economy faltered, and the huge budget deficits caused the national debt to skyrocket, Reagan would repeat over and over,

> The economy has never been healthier, it has never been stronger.

The statements were, of course, untrue because the economy and the federal budget both suffered severely from the Reagan economic policies.

As Reagan's vice president, George Herbert Walker Bush inherited enough goodwill from his association with Reagan to get elected to a first term. However, Bush lacked Reagan's charisma and was on probation with the American voters from the day he took office. If he were to have any chance of being reelected to a second term, he would have to turn the economy around. But Bush continued with the same failed economic policies that had done so much harm to the economy and the federal budget under Reagan.

CHAPTER SIX

CLINTON AND A RETURN TO TRADITIONAL ECONOMIC POLICIES

After a stormy primary campaign, among a field of what most political experts considered "lightweight" candidates, Bill Clinton, the then governor of Arkansas, was nominated as the 1992 Democratic candidate for President. However, most observers still thought the nomination was not worth having and expected Clinton to serve as the sacrificial lamb for the Democrat party. Some of the losing candidates, and those would-be candidates who had chosen not to run, tended to just write off the 1992 election as a lost cause and set their sights on 1996.

Bill Clinton, however, never saw himself as a sacrificial lamb, and he was determined to become the next President of the United States. The boy from Hope, Arkansas, who had once considered becoming a professional saxophone player, had set his sights on the White House while still in high school. As a delegate to Boys Nation, Clinton met President John F. Kennedy in the White House Rose Garden, and the encounter changed his life forever. He decided to enter a life of politics and public service, and he expected to someday return to the White House as President.

Despite his popularity as a wartime president, Bush soon discovered just how important the economy was to American voters. Ross Perot, a self-made billionaire, entered the race as a third-party candidate and ran a one-issue campaign on deficit reduction. Clinton hit hard on the deficit, but also emphasized the need for a major change in Washington. He convinced enough voters, who were looking for change, to vote for him that he received 43.3 percent of the popular vote compared to 37.7 percent for Bush, and 19 percent for Perot. In terms of the electoral votes, the race wasn't even close. Clinton got 370 votes compared to Bush's 168.

Clinton had promised to reduce the deficit, and he was determined to do so, no matter how unpopular his prescription was with the established Washington politicians. He proposed a deficit reduction plan that included both major spending cuts and higher taxes. There was immediate stiff opposition to the plan because it included higher taxes. The Republican party had benefited immensely from the credit it got from the Reagan tax cuts, despite the fact that the Reagan cuts were the primary cause of the ongoing massive budget deficits. The Congressional Republicans were determined to block any effort to raise taxes.

At the time, I was dumbfounded by the official Republican stand on such a critical issue. When Ronald Reagan entered the White House, the national debt was only $1 trillion. That was the total cumulative debt resulting from budget deficits under all previous presidents, from George Washington through Jimmy Carter. If it took more than 200 years to accumulate $1 trillion of debt, perhaps the problem wasn't as serious as some thought. But, it took Reagan only six years to add another $1 trillion to the debt, bringing it to a total of $2 trillion!

The fact that Reagan added as much to the debt in just six years as all previous presidents had added in 200 years, should have put the entire nation into a state of shock. It sure sent shock waves through my body. From day one of Reaganomics, I began to warn anybody and everybody that our nation was headed toward fiscal disaster. I couldn't understand why others were not as shocked as I was. But Ronald Reagan had so much charisma that people believed him when he said all was well with the economy. So Reagan continued with the same policies during his second term, and George H.W. Bush followed along in Reagan's footsteps. During the 12 years of the Reagan-Bush presidencies, an additional $3 trillion was added to the debt, bringing the total debt to $4 trillion. So Reagan and George H.W. Bush quadrupled the size of the national debt from $1 trillion to $4 trillion in just 12 years.

The Republican doomsayers argued that passage of the Clinton economic plan would wreck the economy. House Minority Leader Robert H. Michel (R-Ill.), portrayed Clinton as a traditional tax-and-spend Democrat who was trying to obscure that truth with "the biggest propaganda campaign in recent political history." One House Republican said the Clinton budget was a "recipe for economic and fiscal disaster," and another one said the package "would put the economy in the gutter."

Congressman Dana Rohrabacher (R.-CA) rose on the House Floor and said, "Mr. Speaker, I rise in strong opposition to the Clinton tax increase, the largest tax increase in American history, which will hit the middle class, bring our economy to a standstill and, in the end, increase the deficit."

Republican Congressman Christopher Cox, also from California, was even more graphic in denouncing the Clinton plan. He said, "This is really the Dr. Kevorkian plan for our economy. It will kill jobs, kill businesses, and yes, kill even the higher tax revenues that these suicidal tax increasers hope to gain."

Senate Republicans were equally harsh in their denouncement of the Clinton economic plan. Senator Robert Dole said, "As the President and Congressional Democrats busily work on the biggest tax increase in the history of the world, the American people are watching, and they do not like what they see. To put it simply, the Clinton tax increase promises to turn the American dream into a nightmare for millions of hardworking Americans."

One of the most emotionally charged debates on the Clinton economic plan took place on the floor of the Senate on April 3, 1993 between Senator Christopher Bond (R-MO) and Senator Robert Byrd (D-WV). The differences in the two senators' assessment of the effects of the economic and fiscal policies during the previous 12 years of Republican rule, and their projections as to how the Clinton economic plan would affect the economy and the budget in the years ahead were like night and day. Excerpts from the Senators' remarks are reproduced from the Congressional Record below.

> Mr. Bond. Mr. President, this debate is about keeping faith with the American people. This debate is about ensuring that the Federal Government does not destroy our economy. We have heard today that the stock market took a heavy hit yesterday and was down, and that consumer confidence is down.
>
> I think I can tell you the reason that confidence is down. I think I can tell you why the markets are saying we are not going to see profits, we are not going to see growth, we are not going to see jobs, because this body—appropriately enough on April Fools' Day—passed a budget resolution saying that we would increase taxes a whopping $273 billion. The tax rates that would be jacked up under that resolution may contend that they will raise $273 billion. But we have learned something about taxes, and that is that taxes discourage economic activity.
>
> If you look at the economic game plan that President Clinton has asked for and that the majority in both Houses have adopted, the economic game plan is a recipe for disaster. This so-called stimulus package, which I think is more appropriately labeled an "emergency deficit increase package," is going in exactly the opposite direction of what is needed.
>
> But with 273 billion dollars' worth of tax increases, the Clinton plan, endorsed by this body, turns back up again and, by the year 2000, the deficit is back up to $300 billion a year...
>
> Our leader, Senator Dole, with our Budget Committee leader, Senator Domenici, presented an alternative budget deficit reduction plan that would save more than the Clinton

budget adopted by this body would save, and they did it without increasing taxes. ...

...At some point, the Government is not going to be able to finance its debt. We are essentially going to be bankrupt.

But, in any event, we are going to be putting a tremendous burden on our children and our children's children. They are going to have to pay taxes on that. They are not going to enjoy the standard of living we have, or certainly the standard of living we would like to see them have, because our increased taxes in the budget resolution— the increases in spending there, plus the increased spending that is proposed in this package before us—will go on to their credit cards. And that is a dirty trick.

I see many young people coming to Washington, full of hope, full of optimism. I am embarrassed to tell them that we have already put $4 trillion of debt on their credit cards.

And during the first—and I trust the only—Clinton . administration, we would add another $1.25 trillion to that debt. The Republican Members of this body are united. We have fought to bring some economic sense out of our current budget. We have said: "Cut the additional spending. Don't jack up taxes, particularly when they are going to kill jobs."
...

...We talk about 7 percent unemployment. I believe that the taxes in this measure will drive that unemployment figure even higher, and thus add to the deficit. Spending, if it is left unchecked, is going to drive the deficit back up even with taxes. We believe the time has come to get serious about the deficit. And the only way to get serious is to cut spending.
...The American people are tired of the politics of the past, where Congress continued to vote more and more money without regard to revenues. The tax-and-spend philosophy has not worked. We are attempting to keep faith with the American people who thought we would get a handle on spending.

> If we spend money now, and more money that the
> Government does not have, we will leave the bill for
> someone else down the road—and that is our children.
>   Mr. President, there is much more that could be said
> about this, but I know others want to speak.

Senator Bond painted a very scary picture of what would happen to the American economy and the federal budget if President Clinton's economic package was enacted into law, and he didn't even hint at a link between the Reagan tax cuts and the soaring budget deficits. Senator Byrd, however saw both the past and the future through very different lenses than Senator Bond.

Excerpts from Senator Byrd's remarks are reproduced below.

> Mr. Byrd. Mr. President, the distinguished Senator said the
> time has come to get serious about the deficit. Mr.
> President, let us go back over the past 12 years and talk
> about this deficit that the distinguished Senator has said the
> time has come to get serious about.
>
> Up until the first fiscal year for which Mr. Reagan was
> responsible, there had been no triple-digit billion-dollar
> deficit. Throughout the previous 39 administrations and the
> previous 192 years of history, this country had never run a
> triple-digit billion-dollar deficit.
>
> We had gotten into some double-digit billion-dollar
> deficits under Mr. Ford, $70 billion, $50 billion the next
> year; under Mr. Carter, $55 billion, $38 billion, $73 billion,
> and $74 billion.
>
> Then came the Reagan era. The first fiscal year for
> which Mr. Reagan was responsible, a $120 billion deficit.
> Never heard of before; unheard of before.
>
> The next year, $208 billion; the next year, $186 billion;
> the next year, $222 billion; the next year; $238 billion; the

next year, $169 billion; the next year, $194 billion; the next year, $250 billion; the next year, $278 billion.

That is the first fiscal year for which Mr. Bush was responsible. He had been trained very well under Mr. Reagan, his predecessor.

So in his first fiscal year for which he was responsible, a $278 billion deficit; the next year, $322 billion; the next year, $340 billion; and the next year, $352 billion.

Now, Mr. President, we hear all of this palavering about the deficit; the time has come to get serious about the deficit. After all of this?

Our new President is trying to get serious. He has just been in office 73 days. He has sent up a package, which is a well-balanced package. It is composed of three elements: deficit reduction, long-term investment in infrastructure, and short-term jobs investment. That is what the bill before the Senate does.

Now, the distinguished Senator from Missouri says, and I am quoting him: "The tax-and-spend philosophy will not work."

Well, Mr. President, what I have just shown about this chart concerning the Federal deficits, fiscal years 1979-93— there are the deficits. We are told now that the tax and spend philosophy will not work. Under the Reagan administration, under the Bush administration, we were following a borrow and spend philosophy, a borrow and spend philosophy.

Mr. President, what happened to the total debt as a result of these deficits? When we run deficits, we increase the debt. We are talking about the last 12 years. We are not talking about the previous 192 years in this Republic's history, during which time the country ran up a total of $932 billion in debt; $932 billion. Less *than $1* trillion. But because of the budgets that occurred during the Reagan and Bush years, the triple-digit billion-dollar deficits, we ran up a debt of $4,114 billion as of March 1, 1993.

So when the distinguished Senator says he is embarrassed when school children ask him, why do we not do something? What is happening to our economy? He is embarrassed about the deficits; he is embarrassed about the debt; he is embarrassed about the interest on the debt. Mr. President, there it is. Under whose Presidencies did that debt mushroom, like the prophet's gourd, overnight; from less than $1 trillion, from January 20, 1981, when President Reagan . first took office, to $4,114 billion on March 1 of this year?

Tell the schoolchildren about that. Tell them when the deficits occurred. Tell them under whose administration those deficits occurred.

Mr. President, when those schoolchildren talk to the Senator from Missouri he is going to tell them about the interest on that debt, and rightly so. But the interest on the debt when Mr. Reagan took office was $69 billion in that year. And in fiscal year 1993 it is $198.7 billion. Almost $199 billion. Almost $200 billion.

So, Mr President, tell those children—I hope the Senator will not be embarrassed to tell them when those deficits occurred, when that debt quadrupled, and when the interest on the debt rose from $69 billion to almost $200 billion.

That is a hidden tax, $200 billion a year. That is a hidden tax, a hidden tax. And it is caused by those burgeoning deficits that took place over the last 12 years—a hidden tax.

This President is trying to do something about that hidden tax. He is trying to reduce the budget deficits and eventually, in time, to reduce the debt and concomitantly, the interest on the debt. So I just hope what I said will be helpful to the distinguished Senator from Missouri when he faces those children who are—embarrassed about the deficits.

My grandchildren, my two daughters, and my two sons-in-law are embarrassed, too, about the debt. But I tell them how it rose. And the President, this President who has been

in office just 73 days—73 days—is trying to do something
about it. ...

...Let this President have a chance. Give him a chance.

The Clinton economic plan, the 1993 Budget
Reconciliation Act, was passed without a single Republican
vote in either the House or the Senate. Vice President
Gore's tie-breaking vote was required to pass the measure
in the Senate on August 6, 1993, and President Clinton
signed the legislation into law four days later.

Passage of the Clinton economic plan marked a
major historic turning point. It reversed 12 years of supply-
side economics, more commonly known as Reaganomics.
In addition, it committed the nation to a path of fiscal
discipline that ultimately erased the massive budget
deficits. With the benefit of hindsight, let's look at the
economic record of the Clinton administration.

During the Clinton years, the nation experienced the
longest economic expansion in American history. More
than 22 million new jobs were created in less than eight
years, the most ever under a single administration. The
unemployment rate dropped from 7 percent in 1993 when
Clinton took office to 4 percent in November of 2000. The
overall unemployment rate was the lowest in 30 years, and
the unemployment rate for women fell to the lowest rate in
40 years.

In terms of the federal budget, the record $340.5
billion non-Social Security deficit in the last year of the
Bush presidency was transformed into a record non-Social
Security surplus of $86.6 billion in 2000.

The Republicans, who made it clear in 1993 that
they did not want to be held responsible for the results of
the Clinton economic package, began to sing a new tune
when the results turned out to be just the opposite of what
they had predicted. Former Vice President Dan Quayle
probably spoke for most Republicans when he said, "We do

have prosperity, but let's give credit where credit is due. Ronald Reagan started the prosperity we have today. George Bush continued it, and Bill Clinton inherited it."

A close look at the record shows just how inaccurate Quayle's statement was. President Reagan had the worst unemployment record of any modern president. During his first four-year term, the average annual unemployment rate was 8.6 percent—7.6 percent in 1981, 9.7 percent in 1982, 9.6 percent in 1983, and 7.5 percent in 1984. At no other time since the Great Depression of the 1930s . had the unemployment rate ever been as high for a single year, let alone for a 4-year average. The average annual unemployment rate for Reagan's full 8-year presidency was 7.5 percent.

In terms of financial status, the national debt . doubled from $1 trillion to $2 trillion during the first six years of the Reagan Presidency. It was more than $2.6 trillion when Reagan left office, and it had soared above the $4 trillion mark by the time George H. W. Bush's 4-year presidency had ended.

Republicans have sought to deny President Clinton . credit for the deficit reduction and the strong economy during the Clinton years. After all, they opposed his plan and did not contribute even one Republican vote, in either the House or the Senate, to the passage of the plan. Even worse, they were adamant in their predictions that the plan would devastate the economy and make the budget worse.

However, numerous experts, whose opinions were far more important than those of partisan Republicans, gave Clinton high marks on his economic and budgetary accomplishments. As early as the fall of 1994, former Federal Reserve Chairman, Paul Volcker wrote, "The deficit has come down, and I give the Clinton Administration and President Clinton, himself, a lot of credit for that and I think we're seeing some benefits."

On February 20, 1996, Federal Reserve Chairman, Alan Greenspan, said the deficit reduction in the President's 1993 Economic plan was "an unquestioned factor in contributing to the improvement in economic activity that occurred thereafter."

According to the June 17, 1996 issue of *U.S. News and World Report*, "President Clinton's budget deficit program begun in 1993, led to lower interest rates, which begat greater investment growth (by double digits since 1993, the highest rate since the Kennedy administration), which begat three-plus years of solid economic growth, averaging 2.6 percent annually, 50 percent higher than during the Bush presidency."

All the above comments came after only 4 years of the Clinton administration. Any remaining doubt about the positive results of the Clinton economic program should have been erased during the President's second term. During the last year of the Clinton presidency, the unemployment rate was the lowest in 30 years, 22 million new jobs had been created, the poverty rate was the lowest in 20 years, and there was a non-Social Security surplus of $86.6 billion. Compare this to the whopping $340.5 billion deficit during the last year of George Herbert Walker Bush's presidency, and the staggering projected deficit of $467.6 billion for the third year of the George W. Bush administration.

Credit for the strong economy during the Clinton . years, and for the transformation of the budget from massive deficits to an $86.6 billion surplus in 2000, should go largely to the highly talented economic advisors that Clinton surrounded himself with, and ultimately to Clinton, himself, for listening to their advice and acting accordingly.

Just before his inauguration, Clinton held an economic summit in Little Rock, at which business executives, financiers, and academics, one after another, moaned about how huge federal borrowing to cover debt was making capital too expensive to allow industry to grow. Clinton also put together a team of top economic advisers to help him chart a new course. But even more important than appointing talented economic advisers, Clinton was able to understand their advice, and he implemented much of it. Laura Tyson became Chairperson of the Council of Economic Advisers. Bob Rubin, a widely respected financier, became Secretary of the Treasury, and Harvard Economist Lawrence Summers became Under Secretary of the Treasury. All of these people argued that the economic health of the nation required major reductions in the deficit.

Of course, this was not a new argument. Harvard economist, Martin Feldstein, who served as Reagan's Chairman of the Council of Economic Advisers, made the same argument to both Reagan and to the American people. However, Feldstein soon learned that his advice was not going to be taken seriously because it was in conflict with the political objectives of the Reagan administration. President George Herbert Walker Bush also was advised to reduce the deficits by his economic advisers. However, implementing the advice of his economic advisers was in conflict with Bush's political objectives, so he chose to ignore them. Both Reagan and George H.W. Bush gave their own political objectives a higher priority than following sound economic policies. Most likely, President Bush wished he had paid more attention to his economic advisers on the day he was defeated in his bid for re-election by Bill Clinton.

J. Bradford DeLong, an economist at the University of California at Berkeley was quoted in the February 2001 issue of *The Atlantic* as to the difference between Bill Clinton and his predecessors when it came to listening to economic advisers. Mr. DeLong wrote:

The difference between Bill Clinton and his predecessors lies not in the advice that he was given, but in the fact that he had the brains to understand it and the guts to follow through. Lifting the dead weight of the deficit from the economy cost him essentially all his political capital in 1993. And the rewards in terms of faster economic growth have been greater than anyone in 1993 would have dared predict. Economists will argue for decades to come over how much of the high-tech high productivity–growth boom we are currently experiencing is the result of the high-investment economy produced by the elimination of the deficit. It is a welcome change from the previous sport that academic economists played, that of assigning blame for relative stagnation.

Clinton's economic policies were based on the same traditional economic theory that had dominated American economic policy for more than forty years, prior to the election of President Reagan. That theory, usually referred to as Keynesian economics, was named after the brilliant British economist, John Maynard Keynes whose monumental book, *The General Theory of Employment, Interest, and Money*, published in 1936, changed the way economists looked at the economy. Although his theories have undergone substantial refinement and revision, much of modern Keynesian economics is still rooted on the ideas set forth by Keynes.

Keynes argued that government should play an active role in maintaining the proper level of total spending in the economy in order to minimize both unemployment and inflation. He believed that with the proper use of the government's spending and taxing powers, the extremes of the business cycle could be avoided.

The size of the Gross Domestic Product (GDP), which is a measure of the total production of goods and services in the economy, is very important, in addition to the rate of growth of the GDP, because these two factors are the major determinants of the standard of living. If the GDP grows too slowly, or actually declines, there will be an increase in the number of people unemployed, whereas, if it grows too rapidly, increased inflation may occur.

The level of total production, and thus the level of employment, in the American economy is determined by the level of total spending (aggregate demand) for goods and services. American producers will produce just about as much as they can profitably sell. If sales fall off and inventories start to build up, a producer will lay off workers and curtail production to whatever level can be sold profitably. When sales pick up again and demand exceeds the current level of production, the producer will recall laid-off workers and expand production up to the point where production equals demand.

Thus, the key to a properly functioning economy is to maintain the proper level of total spending (aggregate demand), which is made up primarily of consumer spending, investment spending, and government spending. Through its spending and taxing powers, the government can have some control over the level of aggregate demand. If the economy is in a recession, with high unemployment, either increased government spending or increased consumer spending can help the economy to recover. A tax cut that puts additional take-home pay in the hands of consumers will almost certainly result in increased spending. However, it is especially important that the tax cut be temporary, and of the proper amount to stimulate the economy back to full employment without adding significantly to long-term deficits.

Most Keynesian economists believe that the government should aim for a roughly balanced budget over the long run. For example, over the course of the business cycle, the government's total spending should be approximately equal to it's total revenue. During periods of recession, and high unemployment, tax collections will decline, and there will be an automatic increase in government spending for unemployment compensation and similar programs.

However, as the economy recovers from the recession and laid-off workers return to work, there will be increased tax revenue and a decline in spending for unemployment compensation and similar programs. If Keynesian economic policies are followed consistently, there will be deficits in some years, and small surpluses in other years. Hopefully, over a period of years, the two would roughly balance out.

In addition to the automatic changes in government spending and tax collections that occur over the course of the business cycle, most Keynesian economists believe that the government should use temporary tax cuts to stimulate the economy during periods of recession and rising unemployment. What Keynesian economists do not support is large structural changes in the tax system that will lead to large budget deficits for years to come.

Keynesian economists are deeply concerned about the effect that massive federal borrowing will have on interest rates. If businesses and consumers have to compete with the federal government for scarce funds, interest rates will inevitably rise. Higher interest rates discourage both business investment and consumer spending. Thus, ongoing large deficits alone can cause ongoing high unemployment.

President Clinton recognized the validity of Keynesian principles of economics, and he surrounded himself with competent economists who could advise him on proper government actions. The eight years of prosperity, and the transformation of massive deficits into a respectable surplus by 2000 were not accidental. The Clinton administration practiced sound economic policies, and the economy and the American people benefited enormously.

In short, both the budget and the economy were in great shape when Clinton turned over the reins of power to George W. Bush on January 20, 2001. Bush chose to return to the failed economic policies of his father and Ronald Reagan that have very little support among professional economists. America has paid a high price for that mistake and the long- term costs of Bush's actions are immeasurable.

Despite his positive contributions to the economy and the federal budget, President Clinton must be faulted for the role he played in deceiving the American public about the true status of the federal budget. Like both George H. W. Bush, who preceded him, and George W. Bush, his successor, Clinton continued to use the surplus in the Social Security fund to understate the true deficits in the government's operating budget, and, once the budget was balanced and we experienced two years of surpluses, he used the same accounting procedures to overstate the size of the surpluses.

Bill Clinton was the one who gave birth to the budget-surplus myth. Clinton is the one who first proclaimed the "good news" about the federal government having excess money. It was during Clinton's watch that the Social Security Trust Fund surplus first became large enough to more than offset the continuing on-budget deficit. It was President Clinton who announced a $69 billion federal budget surplus in 1998 when there was really a $30 billion on-budget deficit. It was Clinton who told the American people that the nation ran a $124.4 billion surplus in 1999 when every dollar of it except for the $1.9 billion real surplus, was in the Social Security Trust Fund, and was earmarked for funding the retirement of the baby boomers.

To be specific, in 1998, Clinton claimed there was a $69.2 billion surplus in the federal budget when there was actually a deficit of $30 billion in the government's operating budget. Clinton simply took the $99.2 billion Social Security surplus for that year and subtracted the on-budget deficit of $30 billion to arrive at the mythical figure of a $69.2 billion surplus.

In fiscal 1999, the government experienced a real on-budget surplus of $1.9 billion, the first federal surplus in almost 40 years. However, Clinton was not content to just report the real surplus to the public. Instead, he added the $123.7 billion Social Security surplus for 1999 to the $1.9 billion real surplus and reported the combined total to the American public as the actual surplus.

Finally, in fiscal 2000, there was an unprecedented non-Social Security surplus of $86.6 billion. This was really something for Clinton to crow about, but instead of being honest with the public and reporting the actual non-Social Security surplus, Clinton added the $149.8 billion Social Security surplus and reported a surplus of more than $230 billion. Clinton's true record of deficit reduction would have been phenomenal if he had just been honest with the public, and the Budget Enforcement Act of 1990 prohibited Clinton from combining the Social Security and non-Social Security budgets for purposes of reporting deficits or surpluses. But Clinton chose to violate federal law and deceive the American people with regard to the true status of the budget.

It would have been bad enough if this had been the extent of Clinton's accounting mischief. But this was only the beginning. Clinton claimed that the budget surpluses would continue for a far as the eye could see. On June 26, 2000 President Clinton announced that over the next decade, the federal budget surplus would total nearly $1.9 trillion. This outrageous, deliberate lie to the American people was the greatest sin of the Clinton presidency. It dwarfed the alleged personal misconduct that ultimately led to his impeachment.

From that point on, the American people seemed to believe that there truly was excess money in the federal budget, and cunning politicians began building schemes to further mislead the people into believing that surplus money was available for new programs and/or for cutting taxes. Clinton had given birth to a monster, in the form of the budget-surplus myth, which would later enable George

W. Bush to get by with reckless actions that would threaten America's economic and budgetary future.

How could the President of the United States make such reckless claims? How could the American people be so gullible? The $1.9 trillion projected ten-year surplus that Clinton announced on June 26 was more than 2 ½ times what the administration had predicted it would be just three months earlier, in February! How could anybody give any credibility to a projection procedure that yielded a projection that was 2 ½ times as high as it had predicted just three months earlier?

Clinton did signal the dubious nature of this projection by raising the following red flag:

> This is just a budget projection. It would not be prudent to commit every penny of a future surplus that is just a projection and therefore subject to change."

> It would be a big mistake to commit this entire surplus to spending or tax cuts. The projections could be wrong, they could be right.

President Clinton did the country a great disservice with that announcement. He knew how it would be interpreted by the media, and his motives for making the announcement were exclusively political. After 8 years of dealing with the budget figures, he had to know that the projections were definitely wrong. He also knew that whatever the size of any budget surpluses over the next decade, most, if not all, of it would belong to the Social Security fund.

His political motives for making the announcement were twofold. First of all, he wanted to exaggerate just how much the budget picture had improved under his presidency. Secondly, he probably thought the announcement would help Vice President Gore's campaign.

Strangely enough, the announcement probably helped George W. Bush far more than it helped Gore. The cornerstone of Bush's campaign was his proposed large tax cut, and he needed evidence that the cut was affordable. The Bush camp released the following statement in reaction to Clinton's announcement.

> Today's report confirms the accuracy of the conservative estimates Governor Bush used in preparing his balanced budget plan. The report also demonstrates the importance of passing the governor's tax cuts to prevent all this new money from being spent on bigger government.

The Bush statement was absolutely shocking. Did Governor Bush really believe that there was any new money, except that resulting from the higher Social Security taxes that had been specifically earmarked for funding the retirement of the baby boomers? Surely Bush was aware that the United States Government had more than $4.5 trillion in unpaid bills just from the previous twenty years of deficit spending. The younger Bush should certainly have known that his father's administration had spent $1.1 trillion more than it collected in revenue during President George H.W. Bush's four-year term.

Why wasn't George W. Bush trying to find ways to undo the damage done during the Reagan-Bush years by paying down at least part of the debt accumulated during those years of irresponsible deficit spending? Why would he call for additional tax cuts if he truly understood the government's financial condition?

Equally irresponsible were the statements of Vice President Gore. It is easy to understand Gore's motivation. Like George W. Bush, he was trying to ride the budget-surplus myth right into the White House. Gore felt that he had to promise increased spending on domestic programs to get elected, just as Governor Bush believed that his promised tax cuts would get him elected. Both were citing the mythical budget surplus as the source of funds to pay for their promises.

It is hard to understand why President Clinton behaved so irresponsibly with regard to the budget-surplus myth. Despite the many personal shortcomings of his presidency, I do believe that historians will record that President Clinton did pursue sound economic and budgetary policies throughout most of his presidency which left the economy and the federal budget in much better shape when he left office than when he began his presidency. However, he created and fed the myth that the government had excess money when he should have been urging caution and pointing out that there was no surplus money with which to finance either Al Gore's promises or George W. Bush's proposed tax cut.

CHAPTER SEVEN

GEORGE W. BUSH AND
ANOTHER ROUND OF REAGANOMICS

On February 27, 2001, President George W. Bush delivered his first State of The Union address to a joint session of Congress and to the American people. In this speech, he laid the foundation for his plan to enact massive tax cuts that would benefit primarily the wealthiest five percent of Americans. He also skillfully pulled the wool over the eyes of the public through a series of deceptive statements, designed to convince Congress and the public that the coffers of the United States government were overflowing with billions of surplus dollars for as far as the eye could see. To put it mildly, he deliberately misled the public. To put it more bluntly, he lied to the American people about the financial status of the federal government.

Excerpts from the speech are reproduced below:

> Our new governing vision says government should be active, but limited; engaged, but not overbearing. And my budget is based on that philosophy. It is reasonable, and it is responsible.
> My plan pays down an unprecedented amount of our national debt. And then, when money is still left over, my plan returns it to the people who earned it in the first place.
> To make sure the retirement savings of America's seniors are not diverted in any other program, my budget protects all $2.6 trillion of the Social Security surplus for Social Security, and for Social Security alone.
> My budget has funded a responsible increase in our ongoing operations. It has funded our nation's important priorities, it has protected Social Security and Medicare. And our surpluses are big enough that there is still money left over.

Many of you have talked about the need to pay down our national debt. I listened and I agree. We owe it to our children and grandchildren to act now, and I hope you will join me to pay down $2 trillion in debt during the next 10 years. That is more debt, repaid more quickly than has ever been repaid by any nation at any time in history.

We should also prepare for the unexpected, for the uncertainties of the future. We should approach our nation's budget as any prudent family would, with a contingency fund for emergencies or additional spending needs. For example, after a strategic review, we may need to increase Defense spending. We may need to increase spending for our farmers or additional money to reform Medicare. And so, my budget sets aside almost a trillion dollars over 10 years for additional needs. That is one trillion additional reasons you can feel comfortable supporting this budget.

We have increased our budget at a responsible 4 percent. We have funded our priorities. We paid down all the available debt. We have prepared for contingencies. And we still have money left over.

Now we come to a fork in the road; we have two choices. We could spend the money on more and bigger government. That's the road our nation has travelled in recent years.

If you continue on that road, you will spend the surplus and have to dip into Social Security to pay other bills. Unrestrained government spending is a dangerous road to deficits, so we must take a different path. The other choice is to let the American people spend their own money to meet their own needs.

I hope you will join me in standing firmly on the side of the people. You see, the growing surplus exists because taxes are too high and government is charging more that it needs. The people of America have been overcharged and, on their behalf, I am here asking for a refund.

Perhaps never before in history had the American people been played for such fools by their president. Most people know very little about such things as economics and the federal budget, and so they must trust someone else to tell them the truth. Surely they could believe a new president who was asking for their support to be straightforward with them. If he said the government had trillions of dollars of surplus money, it must be true, regardless of how implausible it seemed. And he wasn't the only top official to say so. Both President Clinton and Vice President Gore had spoken of large surpluses.

I was one of many economists trying to alert the public to the "budget-surplus myth," months before President Bush was even elected. Once Bush's election was certain, many economists tried to warn the public that his massive proposed tax cut would be disastrous for both the budget and the economy. But nobody wanted to listen to professional economists when their president was insisting that there was surplus money and promising to give some of it back to the people.

At the time of President Bush's State of the Union address, the United States government owed approximately $5 trillion dollars more than it had owed just twenty years before when President Reagan had taken office. This represented $5 trillion of unpaid bills. Bush's own father had contributed greatly to this massive red-ink spending. During George H. W. Bush's four years as president, the on-budget deficit (excluding Social Security funds) averaged more than $286 billion per year. And when George H. W. Bush left office, the national debt, which had been only $1 trillion at the beginning of the Reagan-Bush administration, had soared above the $4 trillion mark!

President Clinton also ran on-budget deficits during the first six years of his presidency. However, because of the Clinton deficit-reduction package, the deficits declined significantly during each of Clinton's first six years. Finally, in 1999, the deficit was totally eliminated, and there was a tiny surplus of $1.9 billion. In fiscal 2000, the federal budget had a surplus of $86.6 billion. These were the only two non-Social Security surpluses during the preceding 40-year period, and they may well prove to be the only two surpluses that many Americans will see during their entire lifetimes.

The budget returned to deficit territory during George W. Bush's first year in office, posting an on-budget deficit of $33.5 billion in fiscal 2001. The deficit soared to $317.5 billion in 2002, and a record $450 billion for 2003. Thus, instead of paying down the debt as promised, Bush added more to the debt during 4 years than the first 39 presidents, combined, added to the debt during the first 192 years of American history!

George W. Bush should have been in a better position than almost anyone else to know just how dire the federal budget situation was and what a dismal failure Reaganomics had been during the 12 years of Reagan and Bush's father. His father was vice president for 8 years under Reagan, and served four years as President. As the son of the vice president for eight years, and as the son of the President of the United States for 4 years, George W. Bush had access to information not available to many.

With aspirations to be President, himself, someday, the younger Bush must have talked shop with his father and tried to learn as much about the job as possible. Certainly, he had to know that during those 12 years of Reagan and Bush, the national debt had quadrupled. Didn't he have any concern that Ronald Reagan and the elder Bush had added three times as much to the national debt in just 12 years as all the previous presidents in American history had added in nearly 200 years?

He must have shared his father's pain when the elder Bush failed to win re-election. And all he had to do to learn why his father had been defeated was to follow the news. It was the economy and the massive deficits that did his father in, and it was Clinton's promise to reduce the deficits that brought victory to him. Knowing about those massive deficits during the Reagan-Bush years, and knowing how much the national debt had risen in just a few years, how could George W. Bush keep a straight face when he told the American people that the government had surplus money?

There was no surplus money except for the Social Security fund, and Bush had pledged not to touch that money. As for the surpluses in 1999 and 2000, during the Clinton administration, they weren't enough to even offset the 1997 deficit of $103.4 billion, let alone the other Clinton deficits. The surpluses of 1999 and 2000 came at the peak of the business cycle when the economy was in overdrive, and the unemployment rate was at a 30-year low. Only under such conditions did the economy have the potential to generate enough revenue to even balance the budget. Let's remember that those two years were preceded by 38 consecutive years of deficits!

So where in the world did President Bush think there was going to be surplus revenue? The surpluses in the Social Security fund, that would last only a few more years before turning into deficits, were specifically earmarked for payment of the increased benefits that would coincide with the retirement of the baby boomers. And, once again, Bush had echoed Gore's pledge that the Social Security surpluses would be placed in a lockbox not to be used for anything but the payment of Social Security benefits.

There was no way that there could be ongoing surpluses in the non-Social Security budget, as Bush learned when he ran a budget deficit during his very first year in office. The tax structure was barely capable of generating enough revenue to balance the budget in the top phase of the business cycle when all resources were employed and the economy was producing at its maximum capacity. Only rarely, and for short periods of time, is the economy at this stage. At all other times the economy is either in recession or in the process of recovering from the last recession. During such times, the economy is not operating at the full employment level, and experience over the previous 40 years had shown that, in most years, there would be at least a small deficit.

Despite these facts, President Bush told the nation that the government had massive surpluses. He did not use qualifying words such as "projected surplus" or "anticipated surplus." He talked of the surplus as if he already had it locked in a vault. Consider the following statement:

> We have increased our budget at a responsible 4 percent. We have funded our priorities. We paid down all the available debt. We have prepared for contingencies. And we still have money left over.

George W. Bush was talking about make-believe money, but he led his audience to believe that it was the real thing. He and his staff had concocted a make-believe, fantasy-land budget, and they had manipulated the numbers in such a way as to create make-believe surpluses.

He had not yet done any of the things he refers to. Certainly he had not paid down any of the national debt. On the contrary, he would add more than a trillion dollars to the national debt within four years. He would break the lock on the Social Security lockbox during his very first year, and, during his second year, he would still not have enough money to pay the bills after spending all of the Social Security money. And there would never be any money left over, not even play money.

There was no growing surplus, except for the temporary, planned surplus in the Social Security fund. The non-Social Security budget had run deficits in 38 of the past 40 years. How could he say that the government was charging more in taxes than it needed when his own father had run an average non-Social Security deficit of more than $286 billion per year during his four years as President, and

President Clinton had run deficits during 6 of his 8 years as President?

President George W. Bush who was asking for the trust and support of the American people, deliberately deceived them during his very first State of the Union address. He did so in order to pass a massive tax cut that he knew was not in the best interest of the nation or the economy. It was political payback time. Those wealthy supporters who had given so much money to Bush's campaign had to be repaid. Otherwise, they might not be so generous when he ran for a second term.

In addition to misrepresenting the financial status of the federal budget, Bush also misrepresented the potential economic effects of his proposed tax cut. On February 8, in an effort to stampede his tax cut through Congress, Bush suggested that the economy was headed for trouble, which his tax cut could prevent. Speaking at a Rose Garden ceremony, Bush said, "A warning light is flashing on the dashboard of our economy. And we can't just drive on and hope for the best. We must act without delay." The president said his 10-year, $1.6 trillion tax cut would "jump-start the economy," and he argued that swift passage of the tax cut by Congress could make the difference between growth and recession.

Many observers were shocked that a new president, who had been in office less than three weeks, would make such an irresponsible statement and risk spooking the markets and lowering consumer confidence. When Franklin D. Roosevelt became President, during the depth of the Great Depression, he said, "The only thing we have to fear is fear itself," in an effort to calm the public and build optimism. The fields of economics and psychology are so interwoven that if enough Americans come to believe that the nation is about to enter into a recession their behavior will actually cause a recession. People will respond to their fears by cutting back on spending in preparation for anticipated layoffs, and as new orders to factories begin to decline, workers will indeed be laid off.

To use such scare tactics to get a tax cut, which does little to stimulate the economy, enacted into law, is inexcusable for any President. Some observers suggested that Bush also had another reason for making the statement. After the longest economic expansion in American history, during the Clinton presidency, it seemed almost a certainty that a recession would occur some time during President Bush's four years in office. Some accused Bush of trying to speed up the recession so that the economy would have gone through the recession and recovered by the time he had to run for a second term. No matter what the motives, there is little question that Bush's reckless statement did contribute, at least some, to the recession.

The other flaw in his argument was that quick passage of his tax cut would stimulate the economy. Bush's original proposal did little to provide short-term stimulus. It would have provided only $60 in tax relief during the first year for a single earner making $32,000, and only $120 during the first year for a married couple with a $57,000 income. To stimulate the economy in the short-term, you must put money into the hands of those consumers who will spend it. Tax cuts to the very rich will have a very limited effect on consumer spending, because they already have sufficient purchasing power to buy whatever they need.

On the other hand, low-income consumers have many unmet needs, and will likely spend nearly all of any tax rebate they might receive. The $1.35 trillion tax cut bill that ultimately passed on May 26, 2001, did contain some stimulus in the form of tax rebates. These were added by Democrats in Congress who refused to vote for Bush's bill unless there was a provision for such rebates.

Despite Bush's continuing claims that there was plenty of non-Social Security surplus to fund his tax cuts, and despite his pledge not to use any of the Social Security surplus for anything but Social Security, when the numbers were in for fiscal 2001, the government ran a $33.4 billion deficit. The surplus of $86.6 billion during the last year of the Clinton presidency would be the last surplus for a very long time.

The first year's record of Bush's economic and budgetary policies is very significant, because it was not in any way related to the terrorist attack or the resulting wars against terrorism and Iraq. Fiscal year 2001 ended on September 30, just 19 days after the September 11 attacks, so there was not enough time for any effects to be reflected in that year's budget.

It was also very difficult for Bush to blame that first deficit on a slowing economy. It had only been six months since his March 27 speech at Western Michigan University in which he said that his budget allowed for a "softening" economy.

> Tax relief is central to my plan to encourage economic growth, and we can proceed with tax relief without fear of budget deficits, even if the economy softens. Projections for the surplus in my budget are cautious and conservative. They already assume an economic slowdown in the year 2001.

Obviously Bush's budget calculations were way off the mark, either by design, or due to sloppy accounting procedures. As a result, George W. Bush began reaching into the Social Security cookie jar just seven months after he had solemnly uttered the following words in his State of the Union address:

> To make sure the retirement savings of America's seniors are not diverted in any other program, my budget protects all $2.6 trillion of the Social Security surplus for Social Security, and for Social Security alone.

The Social Security trust fund was raided during Bush's very first year in office. I think there is little doubt that Bush knew he would be digging into Social Security before the end of his term, but even he was probably surprised that the need came so soon.

It had been only four months since the $1.35 trillion, ten-year tax cut had been enacted into law with the assurances of the Bush administration that huge surpluses lay ahead as far as the eye could see. In April 2001, the White House projected a surplus of $281 billion for the fiscal year. This projection included both the (off-budget) Social Security surplus, and the on-budget (operating budget) surplus, despite the fact that federal law prohibits including Social Security into the calculation of either deficits or surpluses.

When the final numbers were in, the non-Social Security budget recorded a deficit of $33.5 billion. Since this $33.5 billion deficit in the operating budget had to be borrowed from the planned, temporary Social Security surplus of $160.5 billion, the overall surplus, including Social Security, had dwindled from the April projection of $281 billion to only $127 billion in less than six months.

How could a budget projection be off by $154 billion less than six month before the end of the budget year? It couldn't! The figures that Bush used in April and May to arm-twist his tax cut through Congress had to be rigged numbers, and the administration had to know about the rigging.

By early 2003, it was quite clear just how wrong Bush had been. The non-Social Security deficit for fiscal 2002 had been a whopping $317.5 billion, and a $467.6 billion deficit was being projected for fiscal 2003. The economy had stalled, the unemployment rate had risen to 6 percent, and two million jobs had been lost just since Bush took office. Obviously the huge $1.35 trillion tax cut had affected the economy very differently than Bush had predicted. So what kind of medicine did the economy need in 2003? According to Bush, we needed still more tax cuts. So, in early 2003, Bush called for a large new tax-cut package, including elimination of the tax on dividend income.

Most economists could hardly believe their ears. Bush was calling for more of the same medicine that had already hurt the economy and the budget so badly. But President Bush, who had revealed his lack of understanding of even the most basic fundamentals of economics over and over during his speeches, totally ignored the warnings of the economists and campaigned against them and anyone else who opposed his latest tax cut. Bush travelled around America trying to convince the American public to put pressure on Congress to pass his proposal.

In the years to come, historians will almost certainly have difficulty explaining the action of the Senate on Friday, May 23, 2003. On that date, the Senate voted to raise the nation's debt limit by nearly $1 trillion, less than a week before the Treasury Department was expected to run out of borrowing authority and risk default on the nation's debt. There was nothing extraordinary about this, in and of itself. Congress has been playing the game of putting a meaningless limit on how much the government can legally borrow for decades, and it always raised the limit whenever the government was about to exceed the limit. When Reagan took office, the legal limit on the national debt was less than $1 trillion, but it was systematically raised to accommodate the soaring debt that had exceeded the $4 trillion mark by the end of the Reagan-Bush admini-strations.

What was so extraordinary about the May 23, 2003 vote to raise the debt ceiling was the fact that it came on the very same day that the Senate also passed a $330 billion tax cut. If the financial condition of the United States government was so dire as to require almost a trillion-dollar increase in the debt ceiling, how in the world could any Senator justify voting for a $330 billion tax cut? The notion of financing a tax cut with borrowed money, at a time when the national debt had risen by more than $5.5 trillion, just since President Reagan took office, defies explanation.

The U.S. House of Representatives, in which the Republicans held a much larger majority than in the Senate, passed the bill by a 231 to 200 margin. But the Senate ended up with a 50-50 tie vote. It took Vice President Cheney's tie-breaking vote to pass the bill in the Senate.

It is ironic that President Clinton's deficit-reduction package passed the Senate only by the tie-breaking vote of Vice President Al Gore. After so much damage to the budget by the Reagan tax cuts, Clinton eliminated the massive deficits in just six years. Now, by the same tie-breaking vote of the Republican Vice President, we were sending the budget back into massive deficit territory.

The tax cut of 2003 was the second Trojan Horse that President Bush had sold to the American public. Bush's 2001 tax-cut package was sold to the American people under the guise that the federal government had huge budget surpluses as far as the eye could see with which to pay for the tax cuts. He promised that his 2001 cuts would not bring a return of deficits and that Social Security money would not be used to pay for them. Since Bush had already been proven wrong about the surplus, the return to deficits, and the borrowing of Social Security surpluses by 2003, he could no longer use that argument. Instead, in 2003 he masqueraded a tax cut, aimed primarily at the rich, as a "jobs-creation" bill.

This was certainly a Trojan Horse because the tax cut was not structured in such a way as to create many jobs. A one-time tax rebate to people who would spend it on consumer goods could certainly have created many jobs at only a tiny fraction of the cost of the Bush plan, but the

Bush plan was structured to give tax relief mostly to those in the high-income brackets, and would thus not stimulate much additional consumer spending. Bush knew that the economists were right and that his plan would benefit the rich without creating many jobs. But he misled the public into believing that a tax plan, designed primarily to benefit the rich, was instead really a job-creation plan.

Did President Bush deliberately and knowingly lie to the American people in order to facilitate political goals that were dear to him? This is a very touchy question. Many people believe that, out of respect for the Office of the Presidency, we should not accuse a sitting President of lying, no matter how obvious it is that the President has lied.

Did President George W. Bush lie to the Congress, and to the American public, about the true financial condition of federal finances in order to get his tax cut through Congress? You decide. There is only one possible other explanation for what happened. That is that the President did not have a clue as to what was going on with the federal budget and was deceived by his own advisors into believing that there would be non-Social Security surpluses when, in fact, massive deficits lay ahead for as far as the eye could see.

Take your pick. Either we had an economically illiterate president who could easily be duped about economic matters by his advisors, or we had a president who knowingly and deliberately lied to the Congress and the American public about the financial status of the federal government, in order to get his tax cut passed. Neither explanation gives me any comfort.

Instead of the $86.6 billion surplus during the last Clinton year, George W. Bush had already added $732 billion to the national debt, only slightly less than the $995 billion added to the debt by the first 39 presidents combined.

President George W. Bush engaged in the worst economic malpractice during his first two years of any president since Reagan. Then, beginning in his third year, he went far beyond Reagan to earn the dubious distinction of the most reckless and irresponsible president in history, with regard to economic and budget policies.

President George W. Bush's 2003 tax-cut proposal, like the massive cuts already enacted, did little to stimulate the economy in the short run, but it did a great deal to help the super rich, at the expense of America's future. But there was a big difference, in terms of economic assumptions between the two proposals. The 2001 tax cuts were enacted under the President's assertion that the government had excess money, which should be returned to the people in the form of tax cuts. He claimed that there would be sufficient revenue to finance the 2001 tax cuts without dipping into the Social Security funds and without a return to budget deficits. Of course, these claims were false, and, by 2003, all Social Security reserves had been borrowed and the government was facing massive budget deficits for as far as the eye could see.

For President Bush to call for additional tax cuts to solve the economic and budget problems was like the Captain of the Titanic screaming "More icebergs!" as a solution to his sinking ship. Unaffordable and ill-structured tax cuts are the main reason that the national debt had soared from less than $1 trillion in 1981 to nearly $6.5 trillion in 2003. And calling for more of the same medicine was absurd.

The vast majority of mainstream economists opposed the tax cut because of the negative effects it would have on budget deficits and the economy. A group of more than 400 prominent economists, including ten Nobel Laureates, signed a statement opposing the Bush tax cut. Their statement appeared as a full-page ad in the New York

Times, so there is no way that President Bush did not get their message. The ad stated, in part,

> Regardless of how one views the specifics of the Bush plan, there is wide agreement that its purpose is a permanent change in the tax structure, and not the creation of jobs and growth in the near-term. The permanent dividend tax cut, in particular, is not credible as a short-term stimu-lus,...Passing these tax cuts will worsen the long-term budget outlook, adding to the nation's projected chronic deficits...To be effective, a stimulus plan should rely on immediate but temporary spending and tax measures to expand demand, and it should also rely on immediate but temporary incentives for investment. Such a stimulus plan would spur growth and jobs in the short term without exacerbating the long-term budget outlook.

President Bush deliberately, and knowingly, ignored this public warning by the nation's top economic experts, and went directly to the American public in an effort to get his tax cut passed despite the opposition of the economists, a majority of the American people, and some highly respected Republican Senators. If President Bush had tried to implement his own battle plan for the war in Iraq, despite his lack of military expertise, and over the objections of the top military experts from the Pentagon, the public would have been outraged and they would have demanded that he listen to the experts.

Yet, the President, whose irresponsible economic policies had already done so much damage to the economy, pushed through Congress another economic package that was not based on sound economic principles, and was opposed by top economists. President Bush fired his original economic advisers because they did not tell him what he wanted to hear. In addition, when more than 400 of the nation's best economists made the effort to warn him against the dangerous and irresponsible pathway he was following, he defiantly ignored them also.

President George W. Bush sold his original huge $1.35 trillion, ten-year tax cut to Congress and the American people by claiming that it would be financed by surplus tax dollars. Furthermore, he promised that he would not take any additional money from Social Security surpluses and pledged to put the Social Security funds in a "lockbox", not to be touched.

President Bush and his advisers had no intention of keeping any Social Security funds as reserves in a lockbox. They knew there would not be non-Social Security surpluses to pay for the tax cut. In fact, they knew there was a high probability that there would not be a single dollar of non-Social Security surplus during the George W. Bush presidency.

The tiny non-Social Security surplus of $1.9 billion in 1999, and the more substantial $86.6 billion surplus in 2000, during the Clinton administration, came at a time when the economy was at the peak of the business cycle, with the unemployment rate at a 30-year low, and these two surpluses were the only non-Social Security surpluses in the past 40 years. How could any reasonable person expect to see continued non-Social Security surpluses once the economy headed into recession?

The 2002 non-Social Security deficit was a whopping $317.5 billion. Even after every penny of the Social Security surplus was borrowed and spent, it was still necessary to borrow additional funds. Furthermore, huge non-Social Security deficits, in the range of $300-500 billion lay ahead as far as the eye could see.

If Bush had admitted that he would be using Social Security, payroll-tax receipts, paid by future retirees, to replace the lost revenue resulting from his tax cut that went mostly to the super rich, the tax bill would not have stood a chance of passing, and he knew it. This deliberate deception of the American public, in order to give tax breaks to the class of people who provided him with so much campaign money, put George W, Bush pretty much in the same company as those he so forcefully denounced as "wrongdoers."

CHAPTER EIGHT

TAX CUTS AND JOB CREATION

If you say something that people want to believe often enough, they eventually begin to believe it. For example, back during the days of the budget-surplus myth, the American people were told over and over that the government had huge amounts of surplus money. They were told by Bill Clinton, Al Gore, George W. Bush, and many members of Congress. Journalists just seemed to accept the myth as true so they passed the good news on to everyone who would listen. Almost everybody got into the act, and organizations began running ads lobbying for part of the loot.

The big debate during the 2000 presidential election campaign was how to spend the unexpected manna from heaven. Gore wanted to spend a good portion of it for improved education, health care, and other programs. George W. Bush wanted to give it back to the people in the form of big tax cuts. Almost nobody was asking such questions as: "Is the surplus real? How could it be real? Where did it come from? Why have we never experienced such a phenomenon before?" The American people were like tiny children who wanted so much to believe that Santa Clause was going to bring them lots of goodies, that they failed to question whether or not there really was a true surplus.

Of course, we know today that there was never any significant true surplus, except for the temporary planned surpluses in the Social Security program, which resulted from the 1983 Social Security tax increase. This money was specifically earmarked for the funding of the retirement of the baby-boom generation, and was not supposed to be used for any other purpose. The tiny $1.9 billion non-Social Security surplus of 1999 and the larger surplus of $86.6 billion in 2000, were the only non-Social Security surpluses of the past 40 years, and they were not even large enough to offset the deficits of 1997 and 1998. A $317.5 billion deficit in 2002 made it clear that the nation was again operating deep in deficit territory.

The whole budget surplus fantasy was a hoax against the American people. Essentially, it was a very big lie told by many people. Some of them may have been so poorly informed about the budget situation that they actually believed what they were saying, but not the top leadership. They willfully and knowingly deceived the American public.

Another lie is that tax cuts of any kind stimulate the economy and result in the creation of many jobs. Tax cuts that put money into the hands of consumers who are not buying because they are unemployed, or because they are on a very tight budget, can stimulate the economy and create jobs. However, tax cuts that go to the super rich, who already have almost everything that money can buy, will have little or no positive effect on the economy or job creation. They will, however, lead to large budget deficits and a soaring national debt.

When the economy is in a recession, with high levels of unemployment, the most effective way of giving the economy a boost is to put money into the hands of consumers who make up two-thirds of the total demand in the economy. The simplest and most effective way to accomplish this goal is through temporary one-time tax rebates. For example, a check for $500, might be sent to each American taxpayer, most of whom would probably spend the rebate. Since it is a one-time rebate, and tax rates are not changed, it would have a very limited effect on deficits over the long run. It would give the economy a jumpstart, which is all that is needed to stimulate it out of recession.

If the primary goal of the tax rebate is to improve the economy, and policy makers don't get all caught up in the politics of who should get how much in terms of fairness, a strong case can be made for targeting most of the tax rebate to those people in the lowest income brackets who will spend almost 100 percent of the rebate on consumer goods and services.

As consumer spending increases and new orders begin coming into factories, the employers will begin calling back laid-off workers so they can increase production. When the newly recalled workers begin getting pay checks again, they will increase spending, causing still more unemployed workers to be recalled. This process can continue until the economy is once again operating at the full-employment level. If the first tax rebate is not sufficient stimulus, then another rebate can be used to complete the job.

When consumer demand is high, employers hire additional workers in order to fill the demand. This is the way that jobs get created. The Bush position that you should give tax breaks to businesses so they will create jobs is just plain wrong. No amount of tax relief for businesses will cause them to create jobs if they cannot sell their products. Demand is what creates jobs. If a company has such strong demand for its products that it is turning away customers for lack of inventory, you can be absolutely sure that it will expand its productive capacity to meet the demand, and not a penny of government tax relief is necessary for them to do this.

Tax cuts for the rich may be good politics for a president who gets much of his financial support from such people, but it is lousy economics. Rich people don't have a lot of unmet needs that they will fill only if they get a tax cut. Everything they want, most of them already have, so when the rich get a tax cut they just turn it over to their accountant with instructions to find a good place to invest it. One of those "good places to invest" is with the United States Treasury.

Because of the tax cuts during the Reagan administration, plus those under George W. Bush, the national debt soared. The government must constantly finance and refinance this huge debt by borrowing. Since the government has to finance its deficits, no matter how high the interest rate, it will always be competing with businesses and consumers for funds. This competition tends to drive interest rates up over the long run.

A lot of the money that the rich receive in the form of big tax cuts is loaned right back to the government. Money that was coming in to the government in the form of tax revenue now comes in the form of borrowed money on which interest must be paid. The key point here is that the large tax cuts to the rich play almost no role in the creation of new jobs. For tax cuts to stimulate the economy and create jobs, they must result in new spending for goods and services.

The idea of cutting tax rates permanently at a time when tax revenue falls far short of expenditures is almost suicidal. It makes no economic sense whatsoever. When you jump start your car with another battery, once the engine starts, you remove the secondary battery. Jump-starting the economy should work the same way. You need a one-time jolt in the form of a tax rebate and then the economy takes off on its own. If the first jolt is not sufficient to stimulate the economy back to the full-employment level, you can always give it another jolt with another rebate, but it is foolhardy to cut long-term tax rates unless you are willing to cut long-term government spending by a similar amount. The deficits that result from the tax cuts require additional government borrowing which can drive interest rates up and reduce business investment spending because of the higher interest rates. If this happens, jobs can be lost because of this particular type of tax cut.

The notion that cutting tax rates can result in increased revenue is nonsense. If your boss tells you that he is going to increase your income by cutting your wage rate, you probably are going to see through the gimmick. Given the same number of hours worked, a lower wage rate means lower earnings, whereas a higher wage rate results in increased earnings. Likewise, lower tax rates mean less tax revenue, and higher tax rates mean more revenue.

This can be seen clearly by what happened during the 1980s, after the Reagan tax cut, and what happened during the 1990s, after the Clinton deficit-reduction package, which included higher tax rates. The Reagan tax cuts led to massive budget deficits and a quadrupling of the national debt in just 12 years. The Clinton deficit-reduction package led to a gradual elimination of budget deficits with actual budget surpluses in 1999 and 2000.

George W. Bush then pushed through another big tax cut and we had a $317.5 billion deficit in 2002 and a projected deficit of $457.6 billion for 2003. Forget about the supply-siders theory that cuts in tax rates generate increased revenue. The theory has been tested and the results are indisputable. No amount of fuzzy math can show that lower tax rates resulted in higher revenue than would have been the case if the rates had been left unchanged.

Some die-hard Reaganites present numbers showing tax collections higher a few years after the Reagan tax cut than they were at the time the rates were cut and offer that as "proof" that the tax cuts resulted in higher revenue. Nice try, but they forgot something. Our economy should be growing continuously over time as the population increases and more productive resources become available. With a growing labor force, and more workers paying taxes, there should be a substantial growth in revenue. Even when tax rates are cut, this ongoing growth in the economy will more than offset the tax rate cut and revenue will increase gradually even at the lower rates.

The point is that revenue would have increased a great deal more without the tax cuts. In short, tax revenue did grow in the years after the Reagan tax cuts, but it did not grow nearly as fast as it would have if the tax cuts had not taken place. The revenue did not rise because of the tax cuts. It rose in spite of the tax cuts, because of the general growth in the population and the overall economy.

By the same token, the natural growth in the population and the economy over time also results in higher government expenditures. Unless the growth in revenue keeps pace with the growth in expenditures, budget deficits will occur. It is precisely because that the growth in revenue did not keep pace with the growth in expenditures after the Reagan tax cuts that the huge deficits occurred and the national debt rose from less than $1 trillion, when Reagan took office, to more than $4 trillion by the time George Herbert Walker Bush vacated the White House.

Likewise, it is precisely because of the deficit reduction package implemented early in the Clinton . presidency that deficits were gradually reduced during his first six years and were replaced by surpluses in 1999 and 2000. And it is because of the reduction in interest rates, made possible by the deficit reductions, that the economy was able to experience the longest period of prosperity in American history during the Clinton years.

A few decades down the road, historians will study the record of Reaganomics and the economic record under Clinton, and they will likely conclude that there must have been some kind of mass insanity in America during the transition period between the Clinton presidency, and the early years of the George W. Bush presidency. How else, they will ask, can we explain that after a twenty-year experiment that clearly revealed the results of supply-side economic policies under Reagan-Bush, and traditional economic policies under Clinton, would the nation choose to launch the new century with the plan that clearly did not work.

If the historians look closely enough, they will see that the American people, who were almost totally illiterate in the area of economics, were the victims of unforgivable fraud by the Bush administration. The Bush people lied to the public in order to enact both the 2001 tax cut and the 2003 cut. In 2001, the people were told that the reason for the tax cut was that the government had surplus money, resulting from over-taxation and that the cut would only return the surplus money to the taxpayers. They were assured that there would be no return to deficits and that the Social Security money would not be touched. The big lie in 2001 was that there was surplus revenue to fund the tax cut.

By 2003, it should have been clear to everyone that the 2001 tax cut inflicted serious damage on both the federal budget and the economy. The talk of fantasy surpluses had given way to the reality that we were once again operating deep in deficit territory. So when Bush decided to try to push through another large tax cut in 2003, he knew the public would no longer buy the lie that there were surplus dollars to pay for it. Instead, he would have to concoct a new lie in order to sell the second tax cut.

This time Bush chose to lie to the public about what effect his proposed tax cut would have on the economy and on employment. So he gave his proposal the nickname of, "Job-Creation Program", and sold it as a remedy for the high unemployment. The Bush tax cut was not a job-creation program. It was an attempt to restructure the tax system to favor the rich. Like all such political proposals, in order to make the proposal more palatable, a few crumbs were included that would also benefit lower income families. But these portions were so small that they would do little to stimulate the economy. The bulk of the cut would do little to create jobs.

One of the traits of a truly intelligent and wise man is that he realizes that he can always learn from experts in any field because they have dedicated their lives, and years of study, to that field. It is hard to imagine any person risking his or her future by going against all the accumulated knowledge and the advice of most of the experts in any field. It is the ultimate in outrageous, irresponsible behavior, for a President of the United States to risk the future of the American people by defiantly and deliberately going against the advice of top experts.

Enactment of both the 2001 and the 2003 Bush tax cuts were accomplished only by engaging in fraud against the American people. Fraud is very broadly defined for purposes of both civil and criminal litigation. An excerpt from the article on fraud in *Encyclopedia Americana* is reproduced below:

> Generally fraud involves the intentional misrepresentation of a material fact, resulting in damage to the victim. So defined, fraud may form the basis of a civil action for damages or of a criminal prosecution...Although fraud is often perpetrated by means of actual statements that misrepresent facts, deception that constitutes fraud can be practiced by concealment, by half–truths calculated to deceive, or tricks or devices that mislead the victim. Also, a statement made recklessly without knowing its truth or falsity may, if false, constitute a fraud.

Certainly Bush's actions to push both tax bills through Congress fell under the criteria of fraud as defined above. The President pushed the 2001 tax cut on the basis of alleged large budget surpluses. There were no such surpluses, and the President had to know this by the time his proposal came up for a vote. He was clearly guilty of "intentional misrepresentation of a material fact resulting in damage to the victim." The victim in this case was the millions of Americans who were adversely affected by repercussions of the tax cut.

Bush was equally guilty of fraud in his campaign to get the 2003 tax cut enacted. In this case, he did not claim that there was surplus money to fund it. Instead, he came up with a new lie about the job-creation potential of the cut. He knew that the 400 plus economists who signed the statement opposing the cut were correct in their contention that it would do little to create jobs. Yet, he deliberately set out to undermine the experts and get the tax cut passed based on the lie that it was a job-creation bill.

The Constitution of the United States provides for the removal of a president from office "on Impeachment for, and Conviction of, Treason, Bribery, or other high Crimes and Misdemeanors." The category of "other high Crimes and Misdemeanors" must certainly include major fraud against the American people. President Clinton was impeached for allegedly lying about an affair with a woman. As repulsive as I find such action by a President of the United States, it was a personal matter that couldn't possibly have inflicted as much damage to the nation and its citizens as Bush's fraudulent actions to push tax cuts through the Congress which were clearly not in the best interest of the nation or its citizens.

In summary, the Bush tax cuts of 2001 and 2003 caused massive additional deficits and pushed the size of the national debt to astronomical new levels. The tax cuts created additional inequalities in after-tax incomes, and they did little to create jobs. Bush could have used one-time tax rebates to restore the economy to full employment at only a tiny fraction of the cost of the tax cuts that were passed, and such one-time rebates would have had little negative effect on the long-term budget outlook.

Bush chose to push the tax cuts through, not in an effort to help the economy, but because the tax cuts were an integral part of his hidden agenda to greatly reduce the size and scope of the federal government. Reagan had tried to starve the government into becoming much leaner by cutting off part of the revenue flow with his big tax cuts. However, Reagan's plan backfired. Instead of decreasing spending by the amount of the tax cuts, Congress chose to replace the lost tax revenue by borrowing and increasing the size of the national debt. Instead of the "tax and spend" policies that Democrats were so often accused of, the Republicans chose to launch a new era that would follow the policy of "borrow and spend."

CHAPTER NINE

THE HIDDEN AGENDA .

Ronald Reagan brought about many changes in America and left a legacy of huge budget deficits and a soaring national debt. But Reagan failed to achieve the goal that was probably most dear to his heart—the dismantling of the federal government, as we know it. Reagan hated big government and was determined to bring about a major downsizing. He had a plan that he thought would accomplish that goal. Reagan's plan was to cut taxes by so much that, when the deficits began to soar, Congress would be forced to dismantle major government programs. He would cut off the lifeblood to the social programs he despised so much, thus starving them to death. Reagan made his intentions very clear in his first televised address to the nation on February 5, 1981. Reagan declared:

> There were always those who told us that taxes couldn't be cut until spending was reduced. Well, you know we can lecture our children about extravagance until we run out of voice and breath. Or we can cut their extravagance by simply reducing their allowance.

Reagan seemed to think he could cut government spending by simply reducing taxes and thus cutting back on the government's "allowance," but he underestimated the determination of members of Congress to spend on programs they believed in whether the revenue was there or not. And Reagan was unwilling to cut back on Defense spending. So the reduction in tax revenue, resulting from the big Reagan tax cuts, was not offset by similar reductions in spending. The national debt quadrupled during the Reagan-Bush years, but spending continued, and the deficit during the last year of George Herbert Walker Bush's presidency was an all-time record of $340.5 billion.

With the election of Bill Clinton in 1992, the attempt to downsize the federal government ended. The Clinton deficit-reduction package eliminated the huge deficits, and Clinton actively tried to make government a more responsive servant to the American people. He even pursued a controversial campaign to establish a national health care system at the beginning of his first term, but failed to get it enacted into law.

Al Gore strongly believed that the government should play an active role in improving the lives of American citizens, and, if he had been elected in 2000, we would have seen increased spending on both education and health care programs during his administration. With the election so close that the outcome was ultimately decided by the United States Supreme Court, and given the fact that Gore received more popular votes than Bush, it would be hard for anyone to make a strong rational argument that Bush had a mandate from the people to bring about major changes in America.

Although the scandal in Clinton's personal life cost him a lot of support, the American people continued to strongly support his domestic and economic policies. The Clinton years saw the longest economic expansion in American history, and the huge deficits of the Reagan-Bush years were eliminated. Many political analysts believe that if Clinton had been eligible to run for another term, he would have been elected because of the prosperity that existed during his presidency.

By no stretch of the imagination can the 2000 election be considered a mandate for any major change in United States policy. Thus, it would have been impossible for George W. Bush to launch a direct open campaign to downsize the government. He would not have been able to get the support of either the Congress or the American people for such action. But getting public support for major tax cuts was a different story, and Bush saw this as an alternative route to dismantling big government.

Like Reagan, George W. Bush was no fan of the federal government. Like most conservative governors, George W. Bush, as governor of Texas, came to despise the restraints placed on state government by the federal government, and his decision to seek the presidency must have been at least partly motivated by his desire to trim the size of the federal government. In order to get elected he needed the support of the ultra-conservative wing of the Republican party, as well as the Christian Coalition and other Christian right organizations.

Bush was at the time considered by many members of the Christian right to be their de facto leader. With the resignation of Pat Robertson as president of the Christian Coalition in late 2001, Bush became generally recognized as the leader and spokesman for the religious right. Gary Baur, a religious conservative who challenged Bush in the Republican primary, said,

"I think Robertson stepped down because the position has already been filled. (Bush) is the leader right now. There was already a great deal of identification with the president before 9-11 in the world of the Christian right, and the nature of this war is such that it's heightened the sense that a man of God is in the White House."

Ralph Reed, who once led the Christian Coalition, contended that conservative Christians tended to view Bush's success as part of a Devine plan. "I've heard a lot of God knew something we didn't," Reed said. "In the evangelical mind, the notion of an omniscient God is central to their theology. He had a knowledge nobody else had: He knew George W. Bush had the ability to lead in this compelling way."

Given this historically unique relationship between the President of the United States and the Christian right, whom Bush needed to be re-elected in 2004, the agenda of the Christian Coalition pretty much became the agenda of President George W. Bush. In choosing Cheney as his running mate, and endorsing a Republican national platform that catered to the extreme right wing of the party at the time of the Republican National Convention, Bush satisfied Christian conservatives who had demanded a staunchly social conservative vice president and platform in return for their support. The Christian Coalition announced at the convention that they would distribute 75 million voter guides and mobilize churches to make George W. Bush the next President of the United States.

Bush used the term "Compassionate Conservatism" to describe his right wing agenda. These two words were contradictory. There is nothing compassionate about true conservative ideology. Over the years, conservatives have consistently opposed programs to help the poor and the disadvantaged. They have opposed programs designed to provide greater equality of opportunity. They have favored cutting benefits to the disadvantaged in order to provide tax cuts to the rich, and they have been more concerned about the profits of large corporations than about the incomes of ordinary Americans.

Compassionate Conservatism was just another Trojan horse, another method of deceit to bring about change that the people would not support on its own merits. Bush was determined to impose his own views and those of right-wing conservatives upon the American people no matter how much fraud was required to accomplish the task. In a speech in Jan Jose, California on April 30, 2002, Bush revealed his desire for limited government. Excerpts from the speech are reproduced below.

> We are a generous and caring people. We don't believe in a sink-or-swim society. The policies of our government must heed the universal call of all faiths to love a neighbor as we would want to be loved ourselves. We

need a different approach than either big government or indifferent government. We need a government that is focused, effective, and close to the people; a government that does a few things, and does them well.

There was no mistaking Bush's view of the role of government. When he said, "We need a government that does a few things and does them well," he was signaling his intention to trim the size and scope of government. Bush went on to explain his philosophy of "compassionate conservatism:"

> Government cannot solve every problem, but it can encourage people and communities to help themselves and to help one another. Often the truest kind of compassion is to help citizens build lives of their own. I call my philosophy and approach "compassionate conservatism." It is compassionate to actively help our fellow citizens in need. It is conservative to insist on responsibility and on results. And with this hopeful approach we can make a real difference in people's lives.

Bush's approach was nothing more than having the government turn its back on the most disadvantaged Americans and calling it compassionate. The conservative portion of the approach was taking the money targeted for programs for the poor and giving it to the rich in the form of tax cuts.

So what was the real reason for the huge Bush tax cuts? It was certainly not because they would help the economy or the budget. They would harm both the economy and the budget. It was not because the government had surplus money. The government had never been so much in the red. I believe the tax cuts were a deliberate effort to put the finances of the United States Government in such dire straights that Congress would be forced to dismantle the social safety net. I believe the purpose of the tax cuts was to intentionally create a financial crisis unlike anything the United States had ever before faced. Under such conditions it might be possible for the conservatives to accomplish things that they could never accomplish through the democratic process.

The Reagan tax cuts had created a situation where the tax system was not capable of generating enough revenue to balance the budget under any circumstances. The Clinton deficit-reduction package partially fixed the problem. In 1999 and 2000, when the economy was operating at the peak of the business cycle, with the lowest unemployment rate in 30 years, the nation was able to experience non-Social Security surpluses for the first time in nearly 40 years. However, in 2001, as the economy slipped into recession, the deficits returned.

In short, before George W. Bush took office and began pursuing tax cuts, the tax rates were already insufficient to generate a balanced budget, except under extraordinary circumstances. There was no wiggle room for even small tax cuts. If tax rates had been left as they were, the government would probably still have run deficits in most years. However, those deficits would have been small enough that they would not have posed a major threat to the budget or economic stability. But even a small reduction in tax rates would have almost guaranteed budget deficits in each and every year.

At the time Bush took over the reins of government, the economy was in the best shape ever with unemployment at historic lows. There was still the fact that the national debt had increased from $1 trillion in 1981 to more than $6 trillion by 2001. However, because there were budget surpluses in both 1999 and 2000, the national debt was not growing at the time Clinton left office.

Bush inherited the best economy in American history, and the budget deficits that had plagued the nation since the Reagan administration had finally been brought under control by Clinton. The old expression, "Don't fix it if it ain't broke," applied to the American economy more than ever before as we entered the new century. Yet, Bush seemed determined to break the economy so that it would need to be fixed. Despite widespread opposition, he pushed his 2001 $1.35 trillion tax cut through, promising that it would not mean a return to deficits or the pirating of any of the Social Security surplus.

By 2003, it was clear that both the economy and the budget outlook had deteriorated instead of improving as Bush had predicted. The 2002 non-Social Security deficit was a whopping $317.5 billion, and the projected deficit for 2003 was $467.6 billion. Instead of admitting that he was wrong and calling for repeal of the 2001 tax cut, Bush's prescription was for more of the same medicine that had already been so lethal.

This time there was no claim that the government had surplus money with which to fund the tax cut. Instead, Bush claimed the tax cut would stimulate the economy and create jobs. Bush knew that the proposed tax cut would create few new jobs and that it would lead to even higher deficits. But what did that matter? It would just speed up the impending crisis, which would enable him to dismantle the government social programs he despised so much.

Budget deficits would become so large as to be overwhelming a little farther down the road. An article in the May 29, 2003 New York Times revealed the shocking results of a study commissioned by the United States Treasury that showed the United States was facing a future of chronic federal budget deficits totaling at least $44,200 billion. According to the article:

> The study's analysis of future deficits dwarfs previous estimates of the financial challenge facing Washington. It is roughly equivalent to 10 times the publicly held national debt four years of U.S. economic output or more than 94 percent of all U.S. household assets.

The study was commissioned by Treasury secretary Paul O'Neill, who was fired by Bush in December 2002. The study was conducted by Kent Smetters, then-Treasury deputy assistant secretary for economic policy, and Jagdessh Gokhale, then a consultant to the Treasury. The study was initially supposed to be part of the budget, but a decision was later made that it would not be included as part of the prospective budget.

The Bush administration chose to exclude the study findings from the annual budget report for fiscal year 2004, which was published in February. At the time the president was actively campaigning for his 2003 tax cut and kept the public in the dark as much as possible as to the outlook for future deficits. It is easy to understand why Bush would not want the public to know about this report. It estimates that closing the gap between revenue and expenditures would require the equivalent of an immediate and permanent 66 per cent across-the-board income tax increase.

The dire predictions of this study which was excluded from the official budget, along with all the warnings from top economists against enacting the 2003 tax cut, should have been more than enough to make Bush reconsider the tax cut, or at least put it on the back burner if he were truly concerned about the future of America and its citizens. Instead, he used pressure tactics, and anything else at his disposal, to get the cut through Congress. Upon signing the bill into law, Bush said:

> We can say loud and clear to the American people: You got more of your own money to spend so that this economy can get a good wind behind it.

It is hard to find any other rationalization for the unaffordable Bush tax cuts other than they will "starve the federal government" and require major spending cuts. Since Defense spending is not a likely candidate for cutbacks, and interest on the national debt must be paid in order for the government to be able to continue to borrow, spending cuts would most likely fall upon Social Security, Medicare, Health Programs and public education.

Since the large surpluses, resulting from the 1983 Social Security tax increase, and specifically earmarked for funding the retirement of the baby boomers were embezzled by the government and spent on other programs, there would be a terrible crunch in both the Social Security and Medicare programs. Unless the government raised taxes in order to repay the massive amounts of money that it had borrowed from these funds, there would have to be major cutbacks in both Social Security and Medicare benefits. One of the most likely scenarios is that these programs would become welfare programs for the most needy Americans. Those who were less needy might lose their eligibility, or at least have their benefits greatly reduced.

The democratic principles of the United States dictate that the public should make the decisions as to what role government should play in their lives and as to what government programs should exist. Conservatives have fought Social Security and Medicare since they were founded, but so far they have not succeeded in their war against these programs because there is wide public support for them. Having been unable to dismantle these programs through the open democratic process, conservatives have turned to underhanded, back-door methods of attacking the programs.

Beginning with the Reagan administration, the conservatives tried to cut back on government funding for these programs by reducing revenue to the point where spending would have to be cut. Reagan promised that his tax-cut program would lead to a balanced budget by 1984, and pledged not to make any major cuts in government services. Such a promise was doomed to be broken. It is not possible to have major tax cuts without matching these cuts with program cuts. Reagan thought the program cuts would come later when revenue became insufficient to fund the programs. But few programs were cut. Instead of the practice of "tax and spend" that Reagan was so critical of, the government adopted a practice of "borrow and spend." The net result was a quadrupling of the national debt in just 12 years.

The deficits were brought under control during the Clinton administration, but George W. Bush almost immediately threw the budget back into deficit territory with his $1.35 trillion 2001 tax cut. Bush then added insult to injury by pushing through the additional $350 billion cut of 2003.

The attempt to eliminate social programs by cutting off their funding source by devious means violates everything that American democracy stands for. It is the people—not the president—who hold the power to decide what programs they want and how much in taxes they are willing to pay for these programs. It is the people, through their elected representatives, who decide the appropriate role of government. And it is the people who have the authority to choose whether to role back the pages of time and return to an era long ago rejected by the majority of Americans, or to move forward to an era where the American dream is possible for more and more Americans.

CHAPTER TEN

THE IMPENDING CRISIS

When Barack Obama became the 44th President of the United States, on January 20, 2009, the nearly three decades of consecutive annual Social Security surpluses was about to end. The surpluses, which were planned and built into the Social Security Amendments of 1983, would end with the small final surplus of 2009.

The original plan was that the surplus revenue would be saved and invested, in order to build up a large reserve with which to finance benefits for the baby boomers, who would begin retiring in 2010. But there was no reserve because all of the surplus revenue had been embezzled by the federal government and spent on wars and other programs. The Social Security program ran a surplus of slightly less than $20 billion in 2009. That was the last surplus, and, in 2010, we began permanent Social Security deficits that will escalate rapidly in the years ahead.

President Obama was not one of the presidents who looted Social Security, but that may be only because there was no Social Security money to loot. Presidents Reagan, George H.W. Bush, Bill Clinton, and George W. Bush managed to make off with every dollar of the $2.7 trillion Social Security reserve fund just like Bernie Madoff successfully stole billions of dollars from his trusting investor clients. Of course, none of the presidents could have pulled off the heist without the cooperation of their respective Congresses.

Although Obama did not participate in the Social Security theft, he continues to participate in the cover-up. I fault Obama for not leveling with the American people about the true status of the Social Security trust fund. I believe that Obama had an obligation to the American people, who elected him President, to expose the great Social Security heist. In a sense, Obama did at lease hint that there was no money in the trust fund.

During the 2011 crisis over raising the debt ceiling, President Obama was asked by a reporter whether or not he could guarantee that Social Security checks would go out on time, even if the debt ceiling was not raised. Here is Obama's response to that question:

> "I cannot guarantee those checks will be mailed. Unless a deal is struck, there may not be enough money in the coffers"

Most people seemed to think Obama's statement was just a political ploy, designed to scare the public. But President Obama was just being honest with the public. Social Security doesn't have a dime stashed away. The Social Security checks could not go out without an increase in the debt ceiling.

On October 3, 2013, during the government shut-down and a threated stalemate over raising the debt ceiling, Obama was even more blunt. He said,

> In a government shutdown, Social Security . checks will still go out on time. In an economic shutdown--if we don't raise the debt ceiling—they don't go out on time.

The president left little doubt that, without raising the debt ceiling, the government cannot pay full benefits. Since the trust fund is empty, and the Social Security tax revenue is not sufficient to pay full benefits, the government simply would not have enough money to pay full benefits.

The Social Security crisis we are now facing became much worse in 2010, when the annual Social Security surpluses of the previous 30 years suddenly turned into permanent annual deficits. The deficit for 2010 was 49 billion, and the gap between revenue, and the cost of paying full benefits, will get larger and larger in the years ahead.

How did the government make up for the $49 billion deficit in Social Security in 2010? It borrowed the money to pay back a tiny portion of its $2.7 trillion debt to Social Security. Seventeen years from now, in 2030, the government would have to borrow $318.7 billion in order to pay full benefits. The nation's finances are under such close scrutiny by credit-rating agencies, the World Bank, and other nations, especially China and our other creditors, that we will be unable to borrow our way out of the Social Security crisis.

Of course, most Americans do not know that the government is now having to borrow money in order to pay full benefits. How could they possibly know? The Social Security Administration, the AARP, and the NCPSSM all have statements on their official websites which tell the public that Social Security has enough money to pay full benefits for at least two more decades.

These statements are outrageous lies. Social Security has nothing but its annual tax revenue, which is insufficient to pay full annual benefits. Social Security does not have $2.7 trillion in the bank. It doesn't even have 27 cents in cash reserves. It has nothing but a pile of worthless government IOUs, which couldn't be sold to anyone, even for a penny on the dollar. Social Security is at the mercy of a government that has stolen $2.7 trillion of its money.

So the impending crisis is upon us now. If the government was willing to raise taxes, in order to get cash with which to repay the stolen money, that would be a potential solution. But the Republicans will not raise taxes for any reason. Neither will they raise the debt ceiling by enough to cover Social Security's needs. There are only three options: (1) raise taxes; (2) borrow more money; or (3) cut Social Security benefits. If we rule out higher taxes and more borrowing, we are left with only one option—cutting benefits.

The nitty gritty of the problem is that Social Security will need to have that $2.7 trillion in surplus Social Security revenue paid back. Unless the money is repaid, Social Security is in deep trouble. That is why there are so many calls for cutting Social Security benefits. That is probably also why President Obama has offered to cut benefits by changing the way inflation is measured for Social Security cost-of-living adjustments.

The theft of the Social Security money is a terrible crime against the American people, and there is no point in mincing words. The government did not borrow the Social Security money. It stole it. And many members of Congress have no intention of ever repaying the money. The American people have been misled by the government, over the past 30 years, about what has been done with their Social Security contributions. Most seem to think the government saved the money and invested it in marketable U. S. Treasury bonds, as it was supposed to do. But that didn't happen.

Not even one dollar of the $2.7 trillion in surplus Social Security revenue, generated by the hefty payroll tax hike of 1983, went to Social Security in any way. Every dollar of the revenue was deposited in the general fund and used to pay for wars and other government programs.

The money was replaced with non-marketable government IOUs. These are nothing more than an accounting record of how much Social Security money has been used for non-Social Security purposes. These IOUs are essentially worthless.

Why isn't the government's embezzlement of the Social Security trust fund money common knowledge today? It's not common knowledge because the government does not want the public to find out that it has been using Social Security payroll tax revenue, as if it were income-tax revenue, for the past 30 years. As bad as the federal budget deficits have been, they would have been much worse if the government had not used Social Security dollars to replace income-tax dollars that were lost as a result of the unaffordable tax cuts under both Reagan and George W. Bush.

So it is all a Big Lie! Both Republicans and Democrats contribute to the lie, because they are equally guilty of misusing the surplus Social Security revenue. If this were a partisan issue, where all the guilt rested with one political party, as was the case with Watergate, the innocent party would have exposed the guilty party years ago. But both Republicans and Democrats have a lot to lose if this becomes public information. Many incumbents in both parties could be voted out of office, if their role in the Social Security fraud were made public.

When I first discovered the Social Security fraud, thirteen years ago, I thought all I would have to do was to tell the media about the terrible scandal. At that time, I believed that freedom of the press in America was a lot more free than it actually is.

It took time for me to come to the realization that most of the mainstream media report only what the government wants the people to know. The turning point in my thinking came as a result of my having the opportunity to talk with a savvy old lawyer who used to work for the Federal Reserve Bank of New York. When I asked the lawyer why the major mainstream news media would not report the story about the looting of Social Security he said without hesitation,

"They've been bought."

I was startled by the lawyer's remark. Surely the government did not control what could and could not be reported by the media. That was too much like the old Soviet Union. This is America, where we send young men and women off to war to fight for our cherished freedom. I asked the man,

"Who bought them?"

"People like Ben Bernanke and Tim Geithner," he responded.

The lawyer then went on to tell me about what he called a "good old boys' network." He explained that most people in high positions in government know other people in high places from previous contacts in college, law school, and past jobs. He said that, if Ben Bernanke does not want certain information to be reported in the news, Bernanke's wish will soon become known to all of the major media. He followed up by saying,

"If Ben Bernanke does not want certain information reported by the news media, it will not be reported."

It has been very frustrating for me to run into one barrier after another while trying to get important information out to the public. When I first discovered the Social Security fraud in 2000, it seemed so horrible to me, that I thought, once ignited, this giant bombshell would explode into the news and spread like wildfire throughout the world. Thirteen years later, because the truth has been concealed so carefully, the bombshell has not yet been ignited.

One of the things that kept me going, throughout all those frustrating years was the story of Australian physician, Dr. Barry Marshall. In the early 1980s, Marshall discovered a link between a certain bacteria and peptic ulcers, which led him to believe that peptic ulcers were caused by bacteria and could be cured with antibiotics. Since medical students had been taught for decades that ulcers were caused by excess stomach acid, and since treatment of stomach acid had become a very big and profitable business, there was much organized resistance to Dr. Marshall's findings.

He was ridiculed by fellow professionals and pharmaceutical companies. Among other things, he was called a "crazy man saying crazy things." In 1998, by which time his treatment for ulcers had become almost universally accepted, he was quoted as saying,

> Everyone was against me, but I knew I was right.

During the decade it took for the medical profession to accept Dr. Marshall's findings, many patients suffered needlessly, and some even died, from an ailment for which a cure had been found.

A similar, more recent, story is the story of Harry Markopolos, an accountant who had figured out that Bernie Madoff was running a giant Ponzi scheme years before Madoff was finally arrested. Markopolis tried repeatedly, over a nine-year period, to warn the SEC about Bernie Madoff's Ponzi scheme. In 2005, Markopolos sent a memo to regulators titled "The World's Largest Hedge Fund is a Fraud." The memo outlined his suspicions in detail and invited officials to check his theories. But the SEC wouldn't take his warnings seriously and took no action. Markopolis expressed his frustrations about not being able to bring down Madoff before he ripped off so many people.

Markopolis said:

"I felt like an army of one, I was a $50 billion failure. I wasn't good enough or smart enough to out maneuver the SEC, the press wasn't listening to me, and I had no other avenue.

In March 2009, Madoff pleaded guilty to eleven federal felonies. He defrauded thousands of investors out of billions of dollars. If the SEC had acted on the suspicions of Markopolos, when he first contacted them, investors would have lost a lot less money.

Patients with ulcers are no longer denied access to the cure discovered by Dr. Barry Marshall. And Bernie Madoff was sentenced to 150 years in prison. But the biggest rip-off in history, the $2.7 trillion of Social Security surplus money that has been used to finance wars, tax cuts for the rich, and other government programs, is still a secret to most Americans. Even as politicians call for cutting Social Security benefits, the government's misuse of the Social Security money is still a big dirty secret.

Obviously, the American people have both a right and a need to know the truth about the Social Security trust fund. The government should admit to the public that it has taken money and replaced it with IOUs.

It is just so wrong for the government to spend Social Security money for non-Social Security pur-poses. Even more troubling, is the fact that the news media and some senior organizations choose to help the government keep its big dirty secret from the public.

This is not just a nightmare that we will eventually wake up from. It is real. The government has stolen all of the surplus Social Security revenue and spent it. The money is gone! And there is only one way to get it back. The people must organize and demand that the government repay the stolen money. Since much of the money was used to finance unaffordable tax cuts for the wealthy, that is the logical place to impose a special tax dedicated exclusively for repayment of the Social Security money.

There are more than 75 million baby boomers (people born between 1946 and 1964) in the United States. Some of them are Republicans, some are Democrats, and some are political independents. Some of the boomers are rich, some are middle class, and some are poor. But there is one thing that all of the boomers have in common. They are all being ripped off by the United States Government!

The boomers are the ones who contributed most of that $2.7 trillion, as a result of the 1983 payroll tax hike. Previous generations were required only to pay for the benefits of their parents' generation. But, because there were so many baby boomers, it was decided that they would have to be treated differently. In addition to paying for the benefits of the previous generation, which was customary, the baby boomers were also required to prepay most of the cost of their own benefits, which was not customary. The extra contributions were supposed to be saved and invested in marketable U.S, Treasury bonds which could later be resold to pay for the benefits of the baby boomers when they retired.

The baby boomers kept their end of the bargain by contributing that $2.7 trillion in extra taxes. But the government did not keep its part of the deal. The government took all that surplus Social Security money and spent it on wars, tax cuts for the wealthy, and other government programs. Not one dollar of the money was ever saved or invested in anything. It was all spent like general revenue, as it came in, over a 30-year period.

Seventy-five million people, if organized, have a lot of political power. That many people can make big waves and a lot of noise. They can change the political landscape. And they have the right to be as politically active as they want to be.

The baby boomers have gotten a bum rap, almost from the day they were born. They were blamed for the need to build additional elementary schools when they were old enough to attend school. A few years later, they were blamed when the number of high schools needed suddenly skyrocketed. They were blamed for the surge in college enrollment when they reached college age. They were blamed for a lot of things. But, they are not to blame for Social Security's financial problems.

So, it is the baby boomers who have the greatest stake in whether or not the Social Security money is repaid. They are the victims of the Social Security theft, and they have the potential power to force the government to repay the stolen money.

Many seniors have put their faith in the AARP and/or the NCPSSM to advise them and to relay the truth about Social Security to the public. As a long-time member of both of these organizations, it pains me to have to say that, like the government, the senior organizations do not seem to want the truth to come out.

As mentioned in an earlier chapter, in early 2004, I sent a letter to, then AARP CEO, William Novelli, along with a copy of my newly published book, *The Looting of Social Security*. I sought the support of Novelli and the AARP in my effort to expose the looting of Social Security. I fully expected them to cooperate with me in alerting the public to the Social Security fraud. I thought they would want the public to know the truth about Social Security. But I was wrong.

In a letter of response, dated Aprail 9, 2004, Novelli scolded me for even daring to call attention to the looting. He did not deny that looting was occurring, but he was adamant about the importance of keeping the public from finding out about the looting. He wrote,

> "Saying that the trust funds have been looted could result in people losing confidence in Social Security, and that is counterproductive."

That letter from Novelli, eleven years ago, was the one and only communication I have had with the AARP leadership. I have tried repeatedly to communicate with them, but they will not respond.

My experience with the NCPSSM has been similar. I have sent copies of my books to them and requested the opportunity to meet with them and discuss the Social Security problem. I have tried to communicate via email, snail mail, telephone and fax. But they will not respond.

I am as much a friend of Social Security as either of these organizations. I believe Social Security is the most successful and most popular program ever created by the federal government, and you don't fix something if it's not broken. Social Security is not broken. Its only problem is that the federal government has embezzled $2.7 trillion of its money. If the government would make arrangements to repay that money, as needed, there would be no need to make any major changes in Social Security in the near future.

I would hope that the goals of the AARP and the NCPSSM for Social Security are similar to my goals. But, if that were the case, why would these organizations have fought every effort I have made to expose the truth? I am a scholar with a Ph.D. degree in economics, and I have been researching and writing about Social Security financing for the past 15 years. Why wouldn't these organizations want to meet with me and compare notes? Why would I be persona non grata for all those years? Why would they not want the public to know the truth about Social Security?

I don't know the answers to these questions. I can only speculate. But, the one thing I know for sure is that both the AARP and the NCPSSM have knowingly and deliberately deceived the American people about the true financial status of Social Security for more than a decade.

Below are quotations from the official websites of the two organizations with regard to the current financial status of Social Security:

> "Without any changes, Social Security will be able to pay 100 percent of benefits for the next 20 years."
> —AARP

> "If Congress does nothing—makes no changes at all—Social Security is projected to deliver full guaranteed benefits until at least 2033."
> —NCPSSM

Members of these organizations, as well as non-members, visit these sites to get what they think is objective information about the true status of Social Security. But both of the above statements are blatantly untrue. To be more blunt, both statements are deliberate lies, and the leaders of these organizations know that the statements are untrue.

The above statements would be true if the great Social Security theft had not taken place. But it did take place! Every dollar of the $2.7 trillion in surplus Social Security revenue, that is alleged to be in the trust fund, was spent to fund wars, tax cuts for the wealthy, and other government programs. None of the money was saved, and, therefore, none of it was invested in real government bonds or anything else.

If you had millions of dollars invested with Bernie Madoff (before he was arrested) you could rightfully say "I have millions of dollars' worth of investments." But now that Madoff is serving a 150-year prison sentence, and you know that most of your money is gone, you can no longer truthfully say that you have the money.

The same is true of the Social Security surplus money. It is true that taxpayers have contributed \$2.7 trillion to the Social Security fund, and, if the money had not been embezzled and spent on other things, we could truthfully say that Social Security has \$2.7 trillion of marketable real assets. If that were the case, the above statements by AARP and NCPSSM would be true. But we now know that the government did not save or invest any of the money in anything. The money was all used for other purposes just as if it were income-tax revenue.

So we cannot truthfully say that Social Security has \$2.7 trillion of reserve assets with which to pay future benefits. That is a lie. Social Security is broke in the sense that it does not have anything except for the worthless IOUs and its annual tax revenue.

The annual Social Security tax revenue has been falling approximately \$50 billion short of covering the cost of paying full benefits. This means that the government has to borrow money, to make up for the shortfall, so that it can pay full benefits.

In order to invest, you must have saved money. If you haven't saved any money, there is nothing to invest. To say that the Social Security surplus revenue has been "invested" in "special government securities," is a big fat lie, being told by the government and also by the AARP and the NCPSSM. The fact that the government put paper IOUs in the trust fund doesn't change anything. These pieces of paper are stored in a fire-proof file cabinet located at the office of the Bureau of the Public Debt in Parkersburg, West Virginia. President Bush visited that office and peered into the drawers of the file cabinet. Bush pointed out that the file cabinet was the closest thing to a trust fund that has ever existed.

I'm not sure why they chose to use a fireproof file cabinet. If the IOUs caught fire and burned, it would change nothing. It would still be true that the government has stolen $2.7 trillion of Social Security money and used it to fund non-Social Security programs.

Today, Social Security is cash broke. It does not have any money, except for its annual tax revenue, and that is not enough to pay full annual benefits even now. Social Security does not have $2.7 trillion in the bank as some claim. It has no cash reserves at all. It would have had $2.7 trillion in the form of marketable U. S. Treasury bonds, if the surplus revenue had been saved, and invested, as was the intent of the legislation. If that were the case, Social Security would have no problems today. It has problems today only because the government failed to save and invest the money. The money is gone!

The AARP and the NCPSSM both try to convince the public that those IOUs in the trust fund are just as good as the marketable Treasury bonds held by China and other American creditors. But they are not at all like the marketable Treasury bonds, which the government was supposed to invest the Social Security surplus revenue in.

U.S. marketable Treasury bonds are traded in markets around the world, and they are default proof. If the United States government were to try to default on a single marketable Treasury bond, it would be seen by the public as a default on all such bonds. That would send shockwaves through financial markets around the world and do permanent damage to the United States' credit standing. These U.S. marketable Treasury bonds are as "good as gold." That is why the Social Security surplus revenue should have been invested in them. If it had been, Social Security would be in great shape today.

The IOUs in the trust fund are nothing like the marketable Treasury bonds. They are not traded in financial markets, and they are not default proof. The government can default on the Social Security debt if it chooses to do so. It would be perfectly legal for Congress to pass new legislation stating that the IOUs are now null and void. If such legislation was passed by both the House and the Senate, and signed by the President, it would become the law of the land. As mentioned in an earlier chapter, in the 1960 case of *Fleming v. Nestor* the United States Supreme Court, ruled that nobody has a "contractual earned right" to Social Security benefits.

The harsh truth is that the United States government is in the worst financial condition that it has ever been in. The national debt which took 200 years to reach the $1 trillion mark in 1981, exceeds $18 trillion today. The tax cuts, under Ronald Reagan and George W. Bush were excessive, and they greatly reduced the amount of revenue that the economy can generate, even when the economy is booming. Having succeeded in getting tax revenue low enough to "starve the beast," and force the cutting of government programs, Republicans will do everything within their power to keep tax rates from going back up. All revenue measures must originate in the House of Representatives, and the Republicans have a large enough majority to prevent that from happening.

It seems highly unlikely that there will be any new revenue legislation in the near future, and Republicans will continue to fight against any substantial increases in the debt ceiling. Without increases in the debt ceiling, the government will be unable to borrow additional money. If these circumstances hold true for the next four years, the only way to reduce the deficit and the national debt will be through additional cuts in government spending. And that almost certainly means cuts in Social Security benefits.

Cash flow is the only true measure of Social Security's financial status. And the cash flow is negative. The AARP and NCPSSM can make believe that Social Security has a backup fund of $2.7 trillion as much as they want, but the harsh reality is that the only money Social Security has is its annual flow of tax revenue, which is insufficient to pay full benefits even for one year. The only way to get additional money for Social Security, other than a tax increase, is for the government to borrow it.

The $2.7 trillion that was supposed to be in the trust fund has been embezzled and spent by the government. And the government is unable, and unwilling, to repay the money. The IOUs are not cash, and there is no way to turn them into cash. They cannot be used to pay benefits, and they have no monetary value.

Some of the Social Security money went to help finance two unfunded wars, but much of the surplus Social Security revenue ended up in the pockets of America's most wealthy individuals and companies, in the form of income tax cuts. Neither the tax cuts of Ronald Reagan nor those of George W. Bush, were funded. So the revenue lost from income tax cuts had to be made up with other tax dollars.

The enemies of Social Security have been saying for the past 78 years, "Social Security is unsustainable in its present form." But they are wrong. As long as the government kept its hands out of the Social Security cookie jar, the program functioned well. And it can function well for another 78 years, with a few tweaks, such as removing the cap on earnings subject to the payroll tax.

Since Social Security benefits have been paid out of the Social Security fund—not the general fund—for the past 78 years, Social Security has not contributed to the deficit or the debt. That is why it is indefensible to cut Social Security benefits as part of the overall effort to reduce the deficit. As long as Social Security operates within its own budget, it should not be tied to the general budget.

In these difficult times, it would be nearly impossible for the government to come up with $2.7 trillion in a lump sum to repay all of the stolen money. But, fortunately, it doesn't have to. It took 30 years for the government to loot the entire $2.7 trillion, so the money can be repaid, in instalments, over the next 30 years.

Where should the money come from? In my opinion, it should come primarily from the same people who benefited most from the Reagan and Bush tax cuts. A small surtax on people in high- income brackets could generate sufficient money to repay the stolen funds without imposing any significant hardship on the taxpayers. The revenue from the surtax would be earmarked specifically for repaying Social Security, and the funds would be deposited directly into the Social Security fund.

This is a workable plan. It would keep Social Security financially sound, while at the same time maintaining the independent nature of Social Security. This action, plus legislation to remove the cap on income subject to the payroll tax, so that everyone would pay a payroll tax on all of their income, just as they do with the income tax, would make Social Security fully solvent for many decades without any other action.

To those who say that it would not be fair to high-income taxpayers to remove the cap on the payroll tax I say, you have been getting a break for the past 30 years while payers of the very regressive payroll tax have been helping pay for your income tax cuts.

I don't know why the AARP and the NCPSSM choose to side with the government instead of with their members. I believe the two organizations owe it to their members, and to the public, to help expose the government's theft of the $2.7 trillion of Social Security money. Why are they helping the government to keep the embezzlement a secret? Why would they show a higher loyalty to Washington politicians than to their members and their Country? It doesn't sound rational. But there is probably a lot that we don't know about relationships between top government officials and the leaders of these two organizations.

For example, while William Novelli was still CEO of the AARP, he did a personal favor for former Speaker of the House, Newt Gingrich. He wrote a glowing preface to Gingrich's new conservative book on health care reform, *Saving Lives and Saving Money*. Since Gingrich is one of the most vocal enemies of the current Social Security system, and supports privatization of the system, massive numbers of AARP members were outraged. AARP members should be outraged today by the fact that their leaders refuse to help expose the great Social Security theft.

If the AARP had been responsive when I first sought their help in exposing the looting of Social Security, the looting could have been abruptly ended and that portion of the $2.7 trillion that has been looted since that time would be safely in the trust fund. But they refused to even communicate with me.

The AARP has it within their power today to undo a lot of the damage they have contributed to in the past. If the AARP would publicly demand that the government find a way to repay the stolen Social Security money, millions of Americans would fall into line and publicly demand that the money be repaid. If the power of those 75 million baby boomers could be harnessed, they could move mountains and save Social Security.

Members of Congress have known about the Social Security theft for decades, and by remaining silent they have contributed to the problem. We need a thorough house cleaning in Washington and a lot of new patriots serving in Congress. Both Republicans and Democrats are equally guilty of this great crime against the American public.

For emphasis, I would like to repeat excerpts from a previously mentioned Senate speech made by Senator

Harry Reid (D-NV) twenty-five years ago, and compare it with Reid's public stance today

On October 9, 1990 Senator Harry Reid expressed his outrage at the misuse of Social Security funds during a senate speech. Excerpts from the speech are reproduced below from the Congressional Record {Page: S14759}.

"The discussion is are we as a country violating a trust by spending Social Security trust fund moneys for some purpose other than for which they were intended. The obvious answer is yes...

It is time for Congress, I think, to take its hands—and I add the President in on that—off the Social Security surpluses. Stop hiding the horrible truth of the fiscal irresponsibility that we have talked about here the past 2 weeks. It is time to return those dollars to the hands of those who earned them....

I think that is a very good illustration of what I was talking about, embezzlement, thievery. Because that, Mr. President, is what we are talking about here...On that chart in emblazoned red letters is what has been taking place here, embezzlement. During the period of growth we have had during the past 10 years, the growth has been from two sources: One, a large credit card with no limits on it, and, two, we have been stealing money from the Social Security recipients of this country."

The same Senator Reid, who made the above points, twenty-five years ago, sounded a very different tone when he appeared on NBC's *Meet The Press* on January 9, 2011. During that appearance, Senator Reed said, "*Social Security is a program that works, and it is fully funded for the next 40 years.*"

No wonder the American people are so confused about the true status of Social Security. Compare Senator Reid's statement on *Meet The Press* with the words of Senator Tom Coburn (R-OK) during a senate speech on March 16 of 2011. "*Congresses under both Republican and Democrat control, both Republican and Democrat presidents, have stolen money from social security and*" *spent it. The money's gone. It's been used for another purpose."*

Social Security is not broken and does not need to be fixed. On the other hand, the federal government is badly broken. Social Security is, however, without any real assets that it can convert to cash. Since it has no marketable bonds that can be sold, it must rely on the government's ability and willingness to redeem IOUs. It doesn't have enough income to pay full benefits. The only money Social Security has is its annual tax revenue. In 2010, Social Security's tax revenue was $49 billion less than the cost of paying full benefits, and the deficits will become larger and larger in the years ahead. What about Social Security's interest income? It doesn't have any. The government "pays interest" by issuing more of those same worthless IOUs, which can neither be sold nor used to pay benefits.

The Social Security Administration, the AARP, the NCPSSM, and many others continue to repeat, over and over, the Big Lie that Social Security has $2.7 trillion in cash reserves, and it can pay full benefits for at least twenty more years without any action by the government. Social Security should have $2.7 trillion in real assets in the trust fund, but it doesn't have a dime.

Hard-working Americans paid enough extra taxes into the system, as required by the 1983 payroll tax hike, to generate $2.7 trillion in surplus revenue. But none of the money was saved or invested in anything. Instead, the money was all embezzled and spent for other purposes by the government. The money is gone just as surely as the daylight is gone when the sun goes down.

INDEX

Allen W. Smith, Professor of Economics, Emeritus, Eastern Illinois University, has been "a voice crying in the wilderness" for more than three decades. During that entire period, he has been battling economic illiteracy and government economic malpractice.

For the past thirteen years, Smith has been trying to expose the fact that our government has embezzled $2.7 trillion from Social Security, leaving the trust fund empty. Dr. Smith is the author of nine books, and he has appeared on CNN, CNBC, and more than 200 radio talk shows. He has a B.S. in Education degree from Ball State University and a Ph.D. degree in Economics from Indiana University.

Made in the USA
Lexington, KY
05 May 2016